Developing a Vision

Recent Titles in Libraries Unlimited Professional Guides in School Librarianship Series
Harriet Selverstone, Series Editor

Developing a Vision: Strategic Planning for the School Librarian in the 21st Century

Second Edition

John D. Crowley

Libraries Unlimited Professional Guides
in School Librarianship
Harriet Selverstone, Series Editor

LIBRARIES UNLIMITED

AN IMPRINT OF ABC-CLIO, LLC
Santa Barbara, California • Denver, Colorado • Oxford, England

Library of Congress Cataloging-in-Publication Data

Crowley, John D. (John Dennis), 1947-
 Developing a vision : strategic planning for the school librarian in the 21st century / John D. Crowley.—2nd ed.
   p. cm.—(Libraries Unlimited professional guides in school librarianship)
 Summary: "This text shows teacher librarians how to become leaders in their schools and apply their unique skills and insight to develop a timely and meaningful vision for the school's library"—Provided by publisher.
 Includes bibliographical references and index.
 ISBN 978-1-59158-891-7 (pbk. : acid-free paper)—ISBN 978-1-59158-892-4 (ebook) 1. School libraries—United States—Planning. 2. Instructional materials centers—United States—Planning. 3. High school libraries—United States—Case studies. 4. Strategic planning. I. Title.
 Z675.S3C85   2011
 025.1'9782230973—dc22   2010053966

ISBN: 978-1-59158-891-7
EISBN: 978-1-59158-892-4

15   14   13   12   11   1   2   3   4   5

This book is also available on the World Wide Web as an eBook.
Visit www.abc-clio.com for details.

Libraries Unlimited
An Imprint of ABC-CLIO, LLC

ABC-CLIO, LLC
130 Cremona Drive, P.O. Box 1911
Santa Barbara, California 93116-1911

This book is printed on acid-free paper ∞

Manufactured in the United States of America

For my beloved wife, Dr. Angela A. Crowley—who inspired me to write this book and who is my enthusiastic partner in our life's journey.

Contents

Acknowledgment

A special thanks to Harriet Selverstone, who urged me to write this book and who patiently coaxed me through the manuscript process.

PART I

Over the past 25 years, I have had the opportunity to be involved in many strategic plans. These plans were for school libraries, public libraries, schools, and school districts. They were always led by consultants with expertise in the planning process. Although each consultant would tend to promote a unique model, they tended to break down to one of two approaches: the marketing model or the classic corporate model. I have seen both models succeed. When the time and resources are available, the classic model is the preferable one. My first book on this topic, *Developing a Vision: Strategic Planning and the Library Media Specialist* (Greenwood, 1994), reflected my experiences helping a school adapt the classic corporate model. Our consultant was very experienced in using this model with major international corporations. We took his wisdom and experience to improve our school. It became an outstanding school, recognized within the state and nation for its innovative practices. I applied this model to the school library, developing a vision that was congruent with the mission and vision of the school.

Subsequent planning experiences exposed me to the marketing model. I call it this because it is employed by many successful marketing consultants. They have shown that although it doesn't carry quite the gravitas of the classic model, it is quite expeditious. I have seen it rolled out in as few as four well-spaced planning sessions. When organized properly and well executed, it can produce amazing results. Given the harried life of the typical school librarian in the 21st century, it is very realistic to acknowledge that the marketing model is the most feasible to employ. However, I will invite the reader to visit chapters of the second part of this book, when appropriate. Ideally, the first part would lead to the second, or at least parts of the second half.

CHAPTER 1

Why Strategic Planning?

What is so unique about developing a strategic plan? Don't we have to plan as part of our normal responsibilities? Can't we just consider our regular duties of running an information literacy program, doing collection development, using the library management software, and collaborating with teachers as enough planning? We might add that the learning Web 2.0 tools would, certainly, qualify us as planners. Unfortunately, as vital as these initiatives are, they are not, in and of themselves, strategic planning. Indeed, because we tend to be the lead on *many* initiatives, such as those just noted, our planning lacks a clear strategy. We attempt to do the best in the time allotted to us. Although time is one of our most precious commodities, we are challenged to set priorities among these initiatives in a time-managed way.

So without a written strategic plan, we are forced to put initiatives on a "time available" basis. Since we are perceived to be a support and service function, many of these initiatives are never given the attention they need. Because we don't consistently communicate our priorities to our superiors, they tend to be unsure of the priorities of the school library. Without a strategic plan, we have nothing to anchor our schedule in the eyes of administrators. We are hard-pressed to negotiate for time and resources if we can't clearly show where we are going. Even if our superiors don't entirely agree with our priorities, they will at least see that we have been thoughtful and deliberate if we engage in a formal planning process. Better yet, if through this planning process we align our priorities with at least some of the priorities of our leaders, they will be more receptive at budget-building time.

Let us make an analogy to planning in our private lives. We are cautioned by our financial advisors to develop a strategy that accounts for the major developments in a typical life. We are usually asked to develop a budget that covers our household's expenses. This includes paying: premiums for the various insurance policies, utilities, mortgage, taxes, savings, and investments. The composition of these accounts will change as our income and needs change, but they are part of a comprehensive plan. Indeed, short of receiving an inheritance, it is almost impossible to plan for our children's college expenses or retirement without a well-developed, goal-delineated plan. It doesn't just happen. It is the fulfillment of long-term and methodical planning. Good household planning forces us to stay loyal to our long-term goals, while acknowledging the everyday needs. All of our resources and energies are not consumed by our daily needs. When our long-term goals are being accounted for, we are maintaining two equally important accounts, long term and short term.

We must bring the same mentality to planning for the school library. If we are always reactive, our long-term goals will never be accomplished. Everything will be short term and in the moment. We will look back on our years of service in terms of attempting to stay afloat in the torrents of initiatives set by others. Just as we could look back with regret for not preparing for our children's education or our retirement, we will look back at careers of unfulfilled initiatives without engaging in strategic planning. Although strategic planning is not a guarantee of eventual improvement of the school library program, anymore than the best financial planning can assure us a predictable retirement, the converse is all but certain.

This book is a description of two types of strategic planning. The first, basic strategic, is an expeditious approach. It is often employed by marketing directors or consultants. It can be done in a few months, sometimes weeks. It is based on a few assumptions:

1. The planners are highly experienced in their fields.

2. There is not enough time to do much in-depth research.

3. There will be participation on the part of all, or at least most, stakeholders.

The second I will call classic strategic planning. This is a protracted, deliberate approach that emphasizes:

1. Thorough and comprehensive research

2. Development of a leadership team

3. Close coordination between the library and school strategic plans

The expeditious type of planning, sometimes called "strategic planning lite," could be a proper run-up or preparation for the more traditional type. However, it can suffice for many school library programs.

CHAPTER 2

Planning Team

Although the school librarian may be the only member of the school library staff who is inclined to develop a strategic plan, we should attempt to involve as many of the staff in some, if not all, of the steps. It is very difficult to foster ownership and understanding if the plan has a single author. Ideally, all the library staff should be invited into the process. Even if some staff members resist initially, we should leave an open invitation. This is especially true for the continue-stop-start stage.

The school librarian can invite as many members as is practical, keeping in mind that smaller groups tend to be the most efficient. However, the school librarian should firmly oversee or champion the entire planning process. After reading this book, there should be an understanding of the major stages of this process. Some stages, including the values statement and continue-stop-start, call for the participation of the whole committee. Others, including the preamble, mission statement, vision statement, current context, critical success factors, core processes, and goals and objectives, could be managed by smaller committees.

The school librarian would do well to invite some members of the school community beyond the library staff. They should include representatives of the faculty, administration, and community. These team members will provide invaluable alternative perspectives during the development of a strategic plan. Eventually, they will become the promoters of the plan, helping to communicate its essential goals. Although it would be wonderful to have people who have a natural affinity toward what we do, it is more important to invite those people who are inclined to value the importance of one or more of these initiatives: 21st-century skills, literacy across the curriculum, and information literacy. Administrators, in particular, tend to perceive the need for any committee that promotes these essential skills. Even if their days are too full to be present at all or most meetings, administrators' eventual support is crucial for the success of the strategic plan.

Considerable thought should be given to building in incentives to participation on the planning team. Care should be given in choosing a pleasant room to meet and providing some enticing refreshments. Since time is such a precious commodity, every effort should be made to have the meetings as brief as feasible. If the committee is so inclined, it can be designed to meet in-person and virtually. This is where the power of blogs, wikis, Google Notes, Google Wave, and social networking, such as nings, can be employed. Although there is a human need to meet, in-person, these Web 2.0 tools have grown very popular because they allow for a high level of interaction that is more convenient for busy people's schedules. Indeed, live meetings and virtual ones can work well together. Live meetings can motivate. Virtual meetings can allow for greater participation and more reflective thinking. Although any and all of these free tools can be employed, nings are the most appropriate. Visit http://TeacherLibrarian.ning.com to get a flavor of the potential of this type of social networking. Joyce Valenza has developed this wonderful site. As this ning exemplifies, serious content can be organized in very appealing and engaging ways. If you do employ this or the other Web 2.0 tools, keep them private (invitation, only) for most of the planning process. The group needs to know that their formative thoughts are for the edification of the planning team and no one else.

An added value of using some of these Web 2.0 tools is that they help us organize and archive the planning process. Since the process will be running parallel to normal duties, it is extremely beneficial to go back to view rich dialog that happened months prior. The Web site can be the ongoing "public record" for the committee. Because sites such as these are collaborative, they contain the context for committee member suggestions and opinions.

CHAPTER 3

Preamble

As the formal first stage of strategic planning, the preamble is a brief description of the existing library program and why we see the need to plan for a changing future. It is an opportunity for us to acknowledge our past achievements and commendations. It, then, moves to a recognition of our need to write goals and objectives. These will enable us to meet the needs of students, who will be living most of their lives in a world that is substantially different than the one we have known. It should assure its readers that our intent, in writing these goals and objectives, is to highlight our recognized strengths, acknowledged weaknesses, identified threats, and continuing commitments. It sets the stage for a planning document that will recognize that no matter how exemplary our program has been, we have no intention of resting on our past achievements.

Recognized Strengths

This is a golden opportunity to list our strong points. Attempt to choose those points that are obvious strengths. They should include sponsors and partners in success. Acknowledging our need to be funded and supported in our initiatives, we should pay homage to the people and institutions that allow us to thrive.

Acknowledged Weaknesses

These weaknesses are the converse of our strengths. They might, as likely as not, be the same people or agencies whom we describe in the recognized strengths. However, we are pointing out areas where they are not as supportive or engaged as would be needed to fulfill our goals and objectives. We have an obligation to expose those weaknesses within our staff that keep us below optimum performance.

Identified Threats

An engaged and involved planning committee will be able to identify at least some major threats to the attainment of our goals and objectives. Budgets are often identified, especially during economic downturns. If we are seen as less than essential to the success of the school, that should be so noted. Remember to think of threats as being either short term or long range.

Our Commitment to the Continued Need to Support

From the inception of the planning process there will emerge a recognition to support certain national, state, and local initiatives, practices, standards, and expectations. The committee should be able to easily come to consensus around those initiatives, practices, standards, and expectations that are the most compatible with the library's core values. Indeed, as the final part of the preamble, this serves as a natural bridge to the next phase of the plan, the values statement.

Sample Preamble

In the first decade of the 21st century, the Joel Barlow High School Library (Redding, Connecticut) has been recognized as exemplary. It has been in the forefront of integration of technology into the curriculum and support of information literacy. It has boldly embraced the challenges of an ever changing world.

As we strategically plan for the next decade of this new century, we must chart a new course for our library. If we were to merely rely upon the beacons of our past recognitions and present reputation, our library would not successfully sustain excellence into the next decade. The world continues to change for us and our students. It mocks complacency, demands agility, exposes weaknesses, reveals opportunity, and presents competition.

So as to successfully guide the Joel Barlow High School Library into the next decade, our plan establishes goals and objectives that address:

Our recognized strengths:

- Board of Education budgetary support
- Administrative support, on a continuous basis
- Talented and versatile staff
- Supportive and caring environment

- Cutting edge use of technology
- A, generally, cooperative student body

Our acknowledged weaknesses:

- A decrease in the literacy of the student population
- An erosion of the student work ethic and intellectual curiosity
- Demonstrated inability, on the part of students, to use free time effectively
- Inability to build an effective system of tracking technology and information literacy skills
- Perceived inability on the part of some staff members to see the "bigger picture" of education

Identified threats:

- Ongoing reduction of library budgets, in favor of technology initiatives
- Belief, on the part of many students and some staff, that the Internet eliminates the need for a library
- State-mandated testing, as a discouragement of those teachers who would want to emphasize information literacy or 21st-century skills
- Aging of the staff

Our commitment to the continued need to support:

- Initiatives from the board of education, administration, and community
- Staff improvement
- Collaboration with the faculty
- Meeting the appropriate national, regional, and state standards in the various literacies (information literacy and reading across the curriculum)
- Involvement in promoting 21st-century skills
- High parental expectations and aspirations for students

CHAPTER 4

Values Statement

Before we begin the steps of strategic planning, it is important, if not critical, to reveal our values vis-à-vis students and programs. These are descriptions of our beliefs about student growth and development, specifically in relation to the school library. Although we are usually in touch with our values, it is important from the outset to make them public. In so doing, we may find that some of our beliefs are not shared by all the library staff. It is better to find these out at the outset. However, it is usually discovered that we share many of the same beliefs and values.

SAMPLE VALUES STATEMENT

The Joel Barlow High School Library values a mutually respectful community in which integrity, intellectual growth, personal responsibility, compassion, and perseverance prevail.

STUDENTS:

Students are central to the values of the Joel Barlow High School Library. Creating a mutually respectful environment in which all students can thrive, the staff focuses on the personal success of everyone. Grounded in a commitment that learning must be continuous for all, staff and students share the responsibility to pursue knowledge.

PROGRAM:

The Joel Barlow High School Library staff values learning in the broadest sense. Its program emphasizes student engagement in the major literacies of today: reading, technology, and information. We believe that high achievement in these areas is essential for success in today's world.

CHAPTER 5

Mission Statement

Simply put, a mission statement is a brief statement of what we are about, as a school library. It should be centered on student learning and describe the unique and critical role the library plays in the success of our clients, the students. It should not be longer than three sentences. It should be general. However, it can be greatly enhanced by a bulleted list of areas of emphasis.

SAMPLE MISSION STATEMENT

The mission of the library is to encourage students to develop the knowledge, skills, and confidence needed to navigate the sea of information.
Thus, we will provide conditions that foster:

- An efficient library, flexible and responsive to students' needs
- An atmosphere of inquiry, encouraging information access
- A program consisting of the skills needed to efficiently and effectively access, extract, synthesize, and present information
- A high expectation of student success in using information
- A diversity of information technologies to allow for differing learning styles and abilities

---

CHAPTER 6

Continue-Stop-Start

Strategic planning almost always begins with a perceived need. Either there is an awareness of the need to improve or an acknowledgement of a growing disconnect between the library's context or culture and its practices. The reasons for entering into the process are not as important as the acknowledgement of the need for change. We, as creatures of habit, have difficulty recognizing the need for change. However, this process can be facilitated by knowing that we are working from an *acknowledgement of our strengths*.

If this process can be summarized, it is an ongoing attempt to:

1. *Continue* what is working and effective, as seen against the mission and vision

2. *Stop* those practices that are diverting us from our main goals

3. *Start* to do the things that will put the library on a path of continuous improvement

Continue

Throughout this process, we must always recognize that there are many things that we do right. Even if we will not be able to focus as much time or energy on them, we cannot afford to jettison what we value. We will discover ways to incorporate what we establish to be core practices. In many respects, these are the easiest practices to discover. They are a combination of the core practices of any good school library and those elements by which we are valued in the eyes of the stakeholders.

Stop

Because we tend to be creatures of habit, stopping those practices that are not mission driven or part of our vision for improvement can, often, be a difficult task. Our daily routine can be cluttered with tasks that were once considered important but have moved into the area of low priority. However, if we persist in performing most of these superfluous duties, we will be frenetic in attempting to "do it all."

15

Start

Finally, we must begin to do the things that are commensurate with our mission and bring us to our vision. Because they will be new functions for us, we must choose to fulfill them in thoughtful and deliberate ways. Although similar to the *Continue* tasks in their importance, these new practices and goals will tend to confuse some of our most loyal allies. Although they are extensions of our core functions, albeit new core, they will befuddle many because they move us into new realms within the school. It is critical that we achieve buy in from administration and some of the faculty. It is just as important that we get support and understanding from our own staff. Since this is the part of strategic planning that is the most critical, it will require the most attention and energy.

SAMPLE CONTINUE-STOP-START

Continue

The Joel Barlow High School Library must:

> Continue to strengthen and update its information literacy curriculum
>
> Continue to maintain high academic standards
>
> Continue to promote diversification in teaching and learning so as to meet the needs of the whole student body
>
> Continue to maintain a creative and flexible environment for students and faculty
>
> Continue to update technology and offer related training and support for staff

Stop

The Joel Barlow High School Library must:

> Stop tolerating inappropriate and nonproductive student behavior
>
> Stop enabling uncommitted students
>
> Stop any unwarranted barriers to student access
>
> Stop making decisions without considering the probable effects on student and staff morale

Start

The Joel Barlow High School Library must:

> Start to create a school-wide ethic that demands individual responsibility for academic pursuits and social issues

Start to address unacceptable student behavior with a fully involved staff and consistent discipline procedures

Start to meet the needs of students with a shift to an emphasis on 21st-century skills

Start to communicate its mission and vision to the greater school community

Start to refresh major technologies on a fixed, multiyear cycle

Start to build a transition plan for replacement of key personnel

CHAPTER 7

Current Context

This is a description of the current library program within the context of the school and the community. It is an acknowledgment of the changes that have had the biggest impact, positively or negatively, on the program. By presenting the context, we root the planning process in reality. By preceding the Vision Statement, it and the site visit reports serve as a reality check.

SAMPLE OF CURRENT CONTEXT

The Joel Barlow High School library recognizes that:

1. We are faced with a changing student profile that challenges the effectiveness of existing structures. Although a minority of the student body uses the library facility effectively, a growing majority chooses to ignore it.

2. The library is well maintained and provides a pleasing atmosphere. The technology is state of the art. It is imperative that these resources be well maintained and updated, since the library is the second-most utilized room in the school (after the cafeteria).

3. Changing needs of and demands on families are reflected in the burgeoning expectations for school support. The library has had to take on some of the tasks that were once the sole domain of the student services department, including career searching and independent study.

4. Technology has had a profound impact on our library. Opening up new opportunities for learning and research, it has challenged the staff and students to grow and change. Overseeing its use and development demands time and vigilance.

5. Community support is essential for the continued success of the library and its programs. Threatened by the community's perception that "real learning" can only take place in a classroom and the adverse effects of the economic downturn on families, we must continue to educate our communities (administrators, faculty, parents, and students), so they understand the importance of investing in an exceptional library.

19

CHAPTER 8

Strategic Themes

Before we can write a vision statement, we must identify the issues that have come to the fore during these initial steps of the planning process. In order to organize our planning, these themes should be thought of as categories or "buckets" into which we will put all the major initiatives. Keeping in mind that we are still going to perform our core processes, these themes are those areas that call for a change in approach. There should not be more that five themes. Since they should be derived from the previous steps, they should be those issues that the planning team sees as needing attention if the library is to move to the next level of excellence.

A member of the planning team should be assigned to be the leader or captain of each of these themes. Although the themes may later be renamed, they should be identified now. Although a structure for collecting research and information on the themes should be decided on, wikis or collaborative tools such a Google Docs, are particularly well suited to the task. They will serve three major purposes:

1. A repository of the history of the research and information gathering

2. A resource for the vision statement and the action plans

3. A consensus building exercise

The planning team should decide on a method of organizing the results of the theme research. Although the theme leader can organize ad hoc teams to gather research and serve as mini planning teams, there is usually not a need to establish a standing committee for each theme.

This is the point at which the theme leaders must determine how they are going to gather information and research for their areas. They have to choose a methodology and a repository for their information gathering. Although there are many ways to approach, the following methods or modalities should be employed:

1. Site visitations to exemplary school libraries, employing an agreed-upon survey

2. Research of the appropriate literature, standards, and Web sites

3. Consultation with acknowledged experts

Site Visitations

The school librarian should be able to identify "Best of the Breed" school library programs. National associations designate certain programs as the best for a given year. These are natural areas to focus on. The most obvious is the American Association of School Librarians (AASL) National School Library Media Program of the Year Award. However, the AASL has other awards that recognize cutting-edge programs, such as the AASL Collaborative School Library Media Award, the ABC-CLIO Leadership Grant, and the Distinguished School Administrators Award. The various state associations of school librarians also recognize outstanding programs. Finally, state consultants are usually aware of the bellwether programs within their states.

Before the programs are visited, either physically or virtually, the questionnaire should be developed. Consisting of a set of questions for each theme, plus an open-ended final question, it is the responsibility of each of the theme leaders to develop questions for their "buckets" or areas. The school librarian should act as editor of the questions, paying close attention that all planning team members understand each one. This is imperative, since the surveys will be conducted by the various members. Thus, the goal is to elicit comparable information that will be vital to the rest of the planning stages.

SAMPLE THEMES

- Literacy

  Three "literacies" are a major responsibility of the Joel Barlow High School Library:

  1. Information literacy

  2. Technology literacy

  3. Reading across the curriculum

  This includes a system of assessment and tracking of these skills.

- Technology

  1. Virtual library—including online databases

  2. Online learning support

- Budget
  1. Board support
  2. Administration's support
  3. Other sources, including local foundations
  4. Internal priorities
- Collaboration
  1. Teacher/library
  2. Partnerships in the community

SAMPLE SURVEY FOR SITE VISITATIONS

Literacy

Describe the library's involvement in each:

1. Information literacy
2. Technology literacy
3. Reading across the curriculum

Technology

Describe how the Internet is used to deliver the services of the library, including:

1. Virtual library
2. Online learning

Budget

Describe how the library has been able to succeed in getting funding from the following:

1. The board of education
2. The administration
3. Other sources, including state, federal, corporate, foundations, and private citizens

Describe how internal budgetary priorities are set.

Collaboration

Describe the best examples of teacher/librarian collaboration.

Debriefing

Once the surveys have been conducted, it is time to debrief the findings. With the captains being especially attentive to findings within their themes or "buckets," the findings should reveal the methods and procedures of the visited school libraries that are yielding successful outcomes. Each of the visiting teams should present its findings. The key to success at this stage is the suspension of judgment. Thus, the proverbial "But that wouldn't work, here" must be avoided. This dismissal should be prohibited in favor of "Let's take elements from each of these reports that may be feasible in the present or the future."

The school librarian will compile findings of these surveys and organize them into six areas:

1. Ready for immediate action

2. Possible within a one- to two-year window

3. Possible within a three- to five-year window

4. Not deployable in the local situation (too unique to the surveyed school library)

5. Not compatible with the mission

6. Beyond the bounds of the present or anticipated budget

We are now at the stage of being able to write the vision statement. Each of the preceding steps has played a necessary role in developing the vision for the school library. We have gathered a planning team, establishing the collaborative nature of good planning. In the preamble, we looked at the existing program and justified the need to plan for a future that will be ever changing. We have exposed our values. We have established our mission. We have looked at our existing program, acknowledging what we have to sustain, refrain from, and initiate. We have described our current context or situation. We have established the major themes or categories, which will be compared to exemplary school library programs. Finally, we have debriefed and organized our findings.

Vision Statement

The vision statement describes where the school library needs to go in the next three to five years. It should be both realistic and inspirational. It should be specific enough that someone could view it many years hence and easily recognize whether or not its main initiatives have been fulfilled or, at least, addressed. It flows from continue-stop-start. It is responsive to the findings of site visitations. It is the basis for all goals and objectives.

Unlike the relatively fixed or stable mission statement, it should be conceived and developed as dynamic and evolving. Finally, it is the public statement of the school library's roles and direction.

The vision of the library should be written with the success of the student as an information problem solver as its central theme. Since a vision statement should show where we are going by showing whence we came, a brief opening statement of what the library has been is a good way to present what it should become.

Although there are varying opinions on whether a discussion of the history of the library is necessary in a vision statement, it is my belief that it is an important element. Since libraries are moving away from being storehouses of materials and toward being learning laboratories or commons, the vision statement should reference this history. This is particularly important since the other people involved in the planning process may not understand the magnitude of the change. If the librarian truly believes that the students of today find themselves in a world virtually flooded with information, the vision statement should present how the library is going to be changed by this information explosion. More important, it should show how its program plays an integral role in helping to prepare students to become knowledge navigators in this sea of information. Fortunately, Web 2.0 tools (blogs, wikis, social networking, etc.) put an emphasis on choice and involvement. Next, there should be a presentation of the role of teachers and the librarians. There should also be a projection of the impact of technology, in general, on the teaching and learning process. All of these elements should add up to a picture of what the library should look like in the future.

The vision statement of the library should show the unique contributions it will give to a restructured or redesigned school. Since it should be considered the information center of the building, the entire school community should be using the library to train (students) or retool (teachers, administrators, and other adults) for the information age. If the student is to be understood as an information navigator or worker, there should be some discussion of what the essential characteristics of this role are. How will the student look in comparison to past standards of a successful learner? A new set of skills has been emerging since the advent of Empowering Learners, Breaking Ranks II, and the Framework for 21st Century Learning. A new set of skills has been emerging since the advent of American Association of School Librarians' *Empowering Learners*, the National Association of Secondary School Principals' *Breaking Ranks II: Strategies for Leading High School Reform*, and the Partnership for 21st Century Skills' *Framework for 21st Century Learning*. The student is seen as much more active and involved. Since he is learning to become a consumer of information, we must look at how he develops strategies to acquire information, extracts the appropriate information, uses the best information, integrates that information into a presentable form, and evaluates the final product. This final stage of information consumption, evaluation, is an essential element of any vision statement. Not only must the individuals using the library evaluate their own work, but the library must evaluate its program. The vision statement should address what a successful program would look like and how it might be judged.

Technology and the role it will play in changing the library cannot be overstated since virtually every major publisher is developing plans for a conversion to digital delivery. Economics alone is going to dictate a shift toward electronics and away from print resources. Add to this the growing acceptance of Web 2.0 tools, and it becomes clear that information may be shared and is not necessarily available only in the library. So profound is the impact of just this one example of technological change that it would be difficult to imagine any vision statement without a significant section on the role of technology.

Since the school librarian plays a critical role in the development of the program of the center, there has to be some elaboration of his role in the process. The vision is, indeed, his notion of what the center must become. Although this vision must fit with that of the school, it will have features unique to the perceptions of the librarian. Site-based planning shows us that only a local team can develop a vision for the school. So too must the librarian develop a unique vision of the center.

The local librarian can take advantage of local, regional, state, and national organizations at this stage. Since other librarians have developed vision statements for their programs, researching other school library vision statements will prove invaluable, since most of us are alone in our buildings. After such networks are in place, different models of visions may be developed. This could have a very significant impact on the evolution of the role of the school librarian as a change agent in the restructuring of American schools.

Sample of Vision Statement

The vision of the future is of a school library that would allow and promote access to information for all ability levels. This center would have as many systems as needed to allow for information to become "transparent," that is, available without a great investment of time and energy. Ultimately, the systems will merge into a unified access program capable of allowing the user to develop a lifelong dialogue with the human conversation.

In the past, emphasis has been placed on the library's role as a repository of books and other materials as well as that of supporting faculty and student use of nonprint media. This tended to combine two fairly dissimilar programs under the umbrella of "media center." The Internet has caused an irrevocable change for these functions. It appears that incorporating artificial intelligence and Web 2.0 tools (blogs, wikis, podcasting, and social networking) will only accelerate the pace of this change. Whereas research techniques (e.g., use of the card catalog) or operation of equipment have been the main thrusts of most library media programs, the ongoing integration of information and the subsequent decrease of the barriers to attainment of that information call for a significant change or paradigm shift.

The combination of artificial intelligence systems and Web 2.0 tools is providing answers to most students' questions. Exciting as this is, it is tempered by the realization that these answers have to be seen as the product of a particular question. The question is more important than the answer. Ask the question slightly differently, and you will get a very different or even contradictory answer. Thus, the new skill has become the ability to ask the informed and intelligent question of the electronic oracle.

If we are in an age of information, we have an obligation to teach our students to navigate through that information. A ship's navigator is not judged simply by his ability to read a compass or chart but by his facility in asking the appropriate questions of his instruments based on his understanding of the weather and the ship's systems and location. Our students must increasingly become aware of their environment (scanning); their own thought systems (metacognition); and where they are going (analysis, evaluation, synthesis, and creation of information). These are the habits of the knowledge navigator. These attitudes and habits are critical for success in the 21st century.

A metaphysical change is taking place. Whereas once we thought of the library media program as centered in a place (library), we are moving into an era of electronic access no longer dependent upon being in a particular facility. Whatever is needed for the student to develop the ability to ask the right questions of the appropriate resources, regardless of location, is the focus of the library's program. The challenge of the school librarian is to act as a change agent in this process. The school librarian remains the professional who is uniquely prepared to meet this challenge.

Critical Success Factors

These are the factors or elements where results are critical to the success of the program. They are those indicators that are typically chosen by accrediting agencies. Although many may be contained in the previous steps, they must be acknowledged as touchstones for the administration's judgment of our program. Before entering in the final stages of a strategic plan, we must ensure that these success factors are incorporated into the plan.

Sample of Critical Success Factors

- The Joel Barlow High School library actively engages in the implementation of the school's curriculum.

- The Joel Barlow High School library provides a wide range of materials, technologies, and other information services in support of the school's curriculum.

- The Joel Barlow High School library ensures that the facility is available and staffed for students and staff before, during, and after school.

- The Joel Barlow High School library responds to students' interests and needs in order to support independent learning.

- The Joel Barlow High School library conducts ongoing assessment, using relevant data including feedback from the school community to improve services and ensure each student achieves the school's 21st-century learning expectations.

- The Joel Barlow High School library is understood to be central to the fulfillment of the school's mission and vision.

- The Joel Barlow High School library aligns its goals and objectives with the mission and vision of the school and district.

Core Processes

There are certain parts of the structure of day-semester-year that have to be acknowledged. They are central to fulfillment of our mission and must be part of our goals and objectives. They are those processes that the school community acknowledges as what the library does. Although some processes are core for the entire school, most are central to the functioning of a well-ordered school library.

Sample of Core Processes

- The Joel Barlow High School library is accessible to all students and staff.

- The Joel Barlow High School library employs effective instructional and management strategies.

- The Joel Barlow High School library incorporates facilities that support and improve the mission and vision of the entire school.

- The Joel Barlow High School library includes the technologies needed to support and improve the educational program of the school.

- The Joel Barlow High School library is involved in curriculum development.

- The Joel Barlow High School library employs professional development for all staff members.

- The Joel Barlow High School library expects staff self-assessment and self-evaluation.

- The Joel Barlow High School library has an inspiring, caring, and dynamic staff.

- The Joel Barlow High School library director recruits and supports an exceptional staff.

- The Joel Barlow High School library staff is responsible for budget development.

- The Joel Barlow High School library communicates its resources and programs to the administration, board of education, and community.

- The Joel Barlow High School library vigilantly maintains a safe, healthy, clean, orderly, and aesthetically pleasing environment.

- The board of education provides the financial and personnel support needed for the fulfillment of the Joel Barlow High School library's mission and vision.

Action Plans

Developing Action Plans

The final sequential step of the planning process is writing the action plans. These ensure that the strategies developed in the planning process are implemented. They outline the tasks required to implement a program, the person responsible for each task, the due date for the completion of each task, and an analysis of the costs and benefits for the specific action plan.

The main intent in writing such plans is to address a particular issue raised in the vision and/or mission statements. Although the bullets of the mission statement should provide the major areas to be addressed in the action plans, it is possible to draw in other areas of focus from the vision statement. All action plans will be subject to the scrutiny of priority, time considerations, resource availability, and feasibility. Therefore, it is best to draft as many plans as can be inspired by the vision and mission statements and limit their numbers later.

Each action plan should include the following sections:

- Issue (from the vision or mission statements) being addressed

- Tangible benefits

- Intangible benefits

- Critical assumptions on which the success of the action plan is based

- Evaluation criteria

- Start date

- Person(s) responsible for its completion

- Date of creation

- Statement of the problem it is written to address

- Action steps, with the person(s) responsible, start date, date due, and date completed

- Resource requirements/cost analysis

Before describing each of the elements of the action plans, it is important to realize how action plans function. An action plan's issue or area of focus is a theme that finds its roots in the previous planning steps. Flowing from strategic themes, the issue an action plan attempts to address (or redress) is first identified at that stage. Let us trace an issue from strategic themes stage, through the vision stage, to the action plan.

In the strategic theme stage, the planning team determined that the erosion of literacy on the part of the average student was an obvious trend. Support for reading across the curriculum was becoming increasingly necessary. Since in the past this had primarily been the domain of the reading teacher, a new approach is required. The problem is increasingly seen as a whole-school issue. A "snapshot" of the building and the district showed that there was a lack of coordination in addressing this issue. Responding to this dissonance, a new approach is warranted. Because of the obvious synergy, it is determined that the school library should play a major role in the solution to this challenge.

Elements of an Action Plan

Issue Being Addressed

As mentioned, the issue is restated, here, in its most specific form: there is a significant decrease in the literacy scores of all high school students, especially those who are below grade level.

Statement of Problem

This is the most important step in the action plan. If you can accurately state the problem to be addressed by the action plan, its solution will be much easier to bring about. When the team is writing an action plan, it would be wise to write the statement of the problem first. The effort involved in attempting to edit it down to an easily understandable sentence is a great opportunity for the group to sharpen its focus.

The statement of the problem for student literacy is: Over the last five years, there has been a significant decrease in the literacy of most students. This is particularly critical for the below-average students. Students are decreasingly able to read and comprehend assigned texts.

Tangible Benefits

Most action plans will have tangible or concrete benefits. In enumerating them, the committee is answering the "why" question, presenting the most provable rationale for proposing this action plan.

The tangible benefits of increased literacy are:

1. A better Lexile match between the average students and their assigned textbooks

2. Lower course failure rate

3. Raised profile of the school library

4. Fewer disciplinary problems

Intangible Benefits

Although some benefits are not quantifiable, they are important and can help sell the action plan.

The intangible benefits of developing strategies to increase literacy are:

1. The school library is more involved in the solution of a critical school-wide issue.

2. A greater sense of community will be developed within the school.

Critical Assumptions

Just as the success of strategic planning, in general, is based on certain critical assumptions, so too is the success of the action plan. It is the estimate of the planning team that without these pieces in place, the plan will not go forward. It is not suggested that there be more than two or three assumptions. However, they should be critical.

The critical assumptions for developing strategies to increase literacy are:

1. The community and board of education will provide the fiscal means to implement this action plan.

2. The administration will endorse the plan and give it a high priority.

Evaluation Criteria

A strategic plan is assessed according to the value and efficacy of the individual action plans. If it did not have such a mechanism, it would not be dynamic. Thus, the action plans should come with built-in evaluation criteria. Since the committee designing the action plan knows the most about its details, it should write the criteria. The method employed should be as concrete and obvious as possible.

The evaluation criteria for developing strategies to increase literacy are:

1. A special committee composed of faculty, administration, staff, and students will be convened.

2. A plan for training will be produced by the above-mentioned committee.

3. Training opportunities will be provided for the faculty and staff.

4. Reports of curriculum changes and classroom practices indicating the use of strategies to increase will be written.

5. An analysis of the results of curriculum changes and literacy strategies will be developed.

Start Date

This is when the first action of the plan is to take place. Actions include not only implementation of the innovation but any of the research that goes into its preparation. If the intention is to start immediately, that should be unambiguously stated. For example, if the start date for the implementation of strategies to increase literacy is this month, preliminary research should begin immediately.

Person(s) Responsible

A person or persons should be named who will oversee the completion of the action plan. It is usually wise to avoid designating a group or committee since accountability is then too easily avoided. If a committee has to be mentioned, use the name of the chair or a prominent member.

Ideally, the assigned person or captain takes part in the action plan writing or design process. Since these plans are going to need enthusiastic and creative shepherding from their coordinators, he should feel a sense of ownership as early as possible. The later the responsible person is brought into the process, the more difficult it will be to bring it to reality. Administering other people's plans is difficult for at least two reasons: the plan will probably not be fully understood, and it will be more difficult to identify with its success or failure.

If we are talking about developing strategies to increase literacy, the responsible person should be the school librarian or reading teacher. Since this person will probably assume the role of in-house consultant, he should be knowledgeable enough to perform this function. Since this person will be training others in literacy strategies, he should be familiar with the most effective strategies to be employed within the various curriculum areas.

Action Steps

The final part of the action plan is the action steps. There should be as many as are necessary to bring the plan to completion. Each step should have: step number column, description of the steps column, "assigned to" column, a start date column, a date due column (if appropriate), a date completed column (if appropriate).

Each of the boxes should contain the following:

Step Number

The step number box is for a simple, sequential numbering reflecting the order of the initiation of the steps. Although there will be some steps that will be completed simultaneously or out of sequence, most will be done in the anticipated order.

There will be seven steps to create and develop a computer network for the school.

Action Steps

The action step box is for a brief (one to three sentences) description of the actual action or performance to take place.

Assigned To

This box names the person(s) responsible for its completion. Participation of the responsible person or captain is important at this phase.

Start Date

A box will contain the start date of each of the steps. Obviously, the first box will have the same date as the start date of the action plan.

Date of Creation

This is important vis-à-vis the start date. It not only shows how long the delay is between the conception and the start, but it supplies a reference point. In strategic planning, it is very important to know when plans are conceived. Since the conditions precipitating and affecting the plan will probably change, it may have to be revised or scrapped when the vision statement is updated. In this case, the date of creation would be the same as the start date.

Date Due

The date due will test the committee's ability to estimate a completion date. Although some steps will be ongoing, most will have end points. The first estimates will probably be inaccurate. However, the experience of seeing the plans develop over a few years will tend to teach the art of estimating time. Thus, each step will have its estimated date of completion.

Date Completed

The actual date of completion is entered in this box. Over time, this box will help the planning team understand which type of tasks tend to be completed within a predicted time and which tend to need more. Since estimating the time required is not always easy, these boxes provide the planning team with important data. When entered into a spreadsheet program, these data help to track the progress of action plans. This will cause the team to review and monitor plans that are not on pace. Some action plans will have to be altered or scrapped because of changes in the external environment. An example might be a new state mandate that runs counter to the direction of the action plan. There could also be a change in the internal world (the school) that causes an elimination of a plan. If, for example, the person responsible for the completion of the plan had his position eliminated, the plan would probably not be completed. Such a plan would probably not have a completion date and would have to be reviewed as soon as possible.

Resource Requirements/Cost Analysis

The two most precious resources of most schools are money and time. Most plans will have to estimate both. Because of the growing scarcity of these resources, estimates should be as realistic as possible.

The money could come from a reallocation of existing funds or a request for new funding. Since budgets are usually proposed 6 to 18 months before the money can be spent, the start date will be different for newly appropriated monies in contrast to reallocated dollars.

The planning committee may need help from administrators on the committee who are familiar with the planning process. Obviously, there will be a need to total the cost of all the action plans and their time requirements before the priority-setting process occurs.

The cost analysis for developing strategies to increase literacy would be $3,000 in the first year ($2,000 for training/staff development and $1,000 for materials); $5,000 in the second year ($3,000 for training/staff development and $2,000 for materials); $8,000 in the third year ($5,000 for training/staff development and $3,000 for materials); $10,000 in the fourth year ($6,000 for training/staff development and $4,000 for materials); and $11,000 in the fifth year ($6,000 for training/staff development and $5,000 for materials).

Communication and Information

Communication and Information are not sections of the vision statement, but they should be considered when developing action plans. Communication is important because the way strategic planning is presented to the greater community will determine its success. The most rational and elegant plan can be rejected by the board of education and the greater community if it is not presented in an understandable form. Critical information must be available to the committee. It includes committee findings and pertinent research.

Communication

Significant attention should be brought to the "marketing" of this action plan. Since it will require the support of the parents, board of education, administration, and faculty, talking points should be developed by the committee members. These talking points should anticipate the objections and push backs that will be faced in attempting to implement this action plan. Although we will be dealing primarily with educators, a volunteer with a marketing background would be invaluable at this stage. The committee should develop a compelling package that would be difficult for a faculty to ignore. Too often the inability to deliver the compelling and obvious reason for adopting an innovation is the cause of its failure to take root.

Information

Since school librarians are usually the information experts within a school community, this function should come naturally. Any important finding, information, and research should be organized by the school librarian and made readily available to the planning committee members. In the beginning, it would be very beneficial to set up a Web site or ning. Although the committee members should be part of the design process, the Web site or ning should contain the major elements of the plan, including:

1. Planning team contact information

2. Preamble

3. Recognized strengths

4. Acknowledged weaknesses

5. Identified threats

6. Values statement

7. Mission statement

8. Continue-stop-start

9. Current context

10. Strategic themes

11. Site visitations (survey results)

12. Vision statement

13. Critical success factors

14. Core processes

15. Action plans

16. Communications (talking points)

17. Critical information (research, finding, test scores, other pertinent data)

CHAPTER 9

Implementation

The most contentious, and potentially difficult, part of the planning process is deciding which plans will receive the most attention and when each will be implemented. This calls for a method of setting priorities. We will need the support, even if it is mostly moral, of all of the planning team members if we are to implement any of the action plans. It is important to bring them into the priority setting process. It is easy to deflate the interest of some of the planning team members by not choosing to immediately implement their action plan. It is, therefore, imperative that they are part of the priority-setting process.

Each action plan should be reviewed by a committee of the whole. The school librarian should lead this process. The decision as to the priority of each action plan vis-à-vis implementation should be based on at least three measurements:

1. Congruence with the mission and vision

2. Feasibility

3. Measurable student outcomes

Congruence with the Mission and Vision

To be consistent will the rest of the strategic planning process, the first screening step is to look at the action plan in comparison to the vision and mission statements. Although such a comparison should have been taking place throughout the planning process, it is possible that an action plan will be proposed that does not seem to receive support from the vision or mission. Unless that plan can be revised through negotiations between the planning team and the action planning committee, it should receive the lowest priority. Plans that are easy to write and inexpensive to enact but do not have any real connection to the vision or mission statements are not going to move the school where it wants to go. Since it will be necessary to review many action plans, it would be useful to rate each of these on a high-priority to low-priority scale. A 6 through 1 scale for this and the other categories will be helpful in determining the final priority order. However, it would not be surprising if all the action plans received high grades for agreement with the mission and vision.

Feasibility

After deciding how closely the action plan conforms to the vision or mission, it will then have to be scrutinized according to its feasibility. Rarely will a school be able to avoid the realities of budgets, time constraints, and unenthusiastic staffs along with other real world considerations. Even if an action plan had a high mark for its synergy with the vision or mission, if it receives a low feasibility rating, it will probably be crippled from the start.

The main elements for judging an action plan's feasibility are:

- *Budget.* How much money does it require to initiate or maintain in comparison to existing or potential resources?

- *Time.* Can this task realistically fit within someone's schedule or can a new position be created?

- *Expertise.* How much specialization is required and does such expertise exist within the present staff?

Measurable Student Outcomes

The final screening process involves what strategic planning for education is intended to address: improvement of student performance. As educators in the 21st century, we shouldn't have to remind ourselves that the public that pays the taxes is looking for results. Although we tend to know that much of what happens in the education process is not readily quantifiable, the spotlight of the media and most politicians will be on tangible results. Therefore, this, the third of the criteria for acceptance of action plans, has to have equal importance with the first two, if not more so.

Having the filter of measurable student outcomes also acts as a safety net for the planning process. Because increases in student learning rarely happen by accident, this criterion should "make or break" the action plan's acceptance. The committee designing the plan should know that concrete results will be one of the three major areas of the assessment of the plan. A plan may seem to be very close to the vision or mission and have a high feasibility rating, but it might have outcomes that are difficult to measure or demonstrate. Having this criterion will increase the vital support this action plan will need from the administration. Strategic planning could look too much like another bureaucratic exercise if most of the action plans do not point to changes that can be seen and measured within a year or two after enactment.

CHAPTER 10

Final Deliberation

The planning committee must come up with a final priority listing. Short of unanticipated largesse, there will be a line below which plans will not make the cut for funding and support. Before dooming a plan to ignominy, there are at least two ways to save it. The first is to combine it, or at least elements of it, with similar plans that have a higher rating. The second is to phase it in over a longer time than originally proposed.

Through creative editing, the planning team can combine parts of action plans that do not receive high enough ratings with a highly rated plan. Although this should be done only when such an addition is seen as strengthening the accepted action plan, it serves a multitude of purposes. It tends to show the planning committees that there are certain shared themes or unities. It allows a particularly exceptional step of an otherwise lowly rated plan to be adopted. Finally, and most important, it tells the committee that wrote the action plan that its thoughts and work are valued.

Action Plan (title):			
Congruence with Mission and Vision			
Feasibility (Budget, Time, and Expertise)			
Measurable Student Outcomes			
Total Score:			

Initiating the Action Plans

Once we have vetted our action plans and initiated them, we need to give more thought to the method of analysis we intend to employ. This would be a good time to bring the action plans to the attention of our supervisors. Since they have to direct their attention to the measurement of student outcomes, their advice will serve multiple purposes. It will make them aware of a focus of the library's program. It will tend to build ownership for the success of the action plan. Finally, it will alert them to the need for resources, especially at budget-building time.

As to the development of a method of analysis, administrators are quite familiar with various approaches. They could make suggestions as to what tool is the most appropriate for the action plan. One of the simplest tools is an online survey. If the district pays for a subscription to survey Web sites, such as surveymonkey.com, the school librarian and/or the planning committee could develop an appropriate survey for teachers or students. Since veteran teachers are usually interested in improving student engagement and performance, they should be able to discern if the innovation employed as a consequence of the action plan is having a positive impact on student learning. Although surveys do not carry the same gravitas as state-mandated assessment results, they can be an important indicator of an innovation that is beginning to take traction.

I developed the following survey for teachers to track the impact of a plan to incorporate the use of one of our subscription services, Facts On File's "Issues and Controversies," into a requirement assignment for all tenth graders. It is a writing and speaking exercise, referred to as "Sophomore Speakout." Each student must write a speech that addresses a serious issue that is of personal concern. Since our state testers often choose from this database when creating a critical writing task, this assignment is designed to teach reading strategies that are needed be able to write an essay that reaches the state standard. Although the outcomes are different, a speech versus an essay, the reading and analytical skills are very similar.

This survey is intended to be given soon after the speeches are graded. It only requires a few minutes of the teachers' time, but it will serve as the first measurement of the success of the innovation. Since this unit will be assigned to all tenth graders, I will be able to see if the teachers' perception of success or failure of this unit coincides with the percentage of students who achieve standard (district's goal) on this part of the Connecticut Academic Progress Test (CAPT). Over the course of two or three years, these two data points should inform us as to whether this teaching unit is promoting student literacy (reading and information) and is worthy of incorporation into the tenth grade curriculum.

SAMPLE SURVEY

1. I found the lesson on using the "Issues and Controversies" database to be time well spent.

   Strongly agree

Agree

Neutral

Disagree

Strongly disagree

2. The eBoard tutorial was helpful for students who were absent or those who needed to review the steps to finding information in the "Issues and Controversies" database.

Strongly agree

Agree

Neutral

Disagree

Strongly disagree

3. This research assignment was good preparation for writing the essay for the Sophomore Speakout.

Strongly agree

Agree

Neutral

Disagree

Strongly disagree

4. This research assignment was good preparation for the Interdisciplinary Writing section of the CAPT test.

Strongly agree

Agree

Neutral

Disagree

Strongly disagree

5. The most helpful part of "Issues and Controversies" was:

Its organization

Its succinctness

Its graphics

Its narrative style

Its keyword section

Its referencing other Web sites

6. The second most helpful part of "Issues and Controversies" was:

Its organization

Its succinctness

Its graphics

Its narrative style

Its keyword section

Its referencing other Web sites

7. The third most helpful part of "Issues and Controversies" was:

Its organization

Its succinctness

Its graphics

Its narrative style

Its keyword section

Its referencing other Web sites

CHAPTER 11

Other Considerations

Annual Goals

Since most school librarians are expected to submit annual goals for the evaluation process, it would be a powerful statement to incorporate one of the action plans into the goal. Indeed, using the analysis of an action plan as a part of professional goal, the school librarian could be a model for the rest of the faculty. Such a goal shows that he is focused on student achievement, knowledgeable in data collection, willing to analyze data to adjust the innovation, and can determine the place of this goal in the long-range plan for the school library. (See Part II of this book to determine ways to build congruence between the library's strategic plan and the school or district's strategic plan.)

Sustainability

The final step in the planning process is the one that is most prone to failure. It is the process of turning the action plans into long-term change. I have found that this is the part of the planning process that calls for the greatest fortitude on the part of the school librarian. Even if the action plans are collaboratively developed, someone has to be responsible for their oversight. Plans will not implement themselves. As the planning team members move on to their normal professional and personal lives, the school librarian will be faced with keeping the action plans moving and vital. There are three supports to promoting sustainability. They are:

1. Relationship among the parts of the planning process

2. Understanding the change process

3. Professional development

Relationship Among the Parts of the Planning Process

The first time through the planning process, it is necessary to go through the various steps sequentially. However, this linear approach is mostly for purposes of learning and team building. Once the planning team has all the steps completed, it is no longer a sequential process. Although elements of the plan, especially continue-stop-start and current context will have to be reviewed and updated, it is not a matter of "returning to go," as in the game of Monopoly. Rather, this and the other steps become subsystems to the process of strategic planning. Just as the various subsystems of the body (circulatory, respiratory, etc.) function simultaneously, so too should the elements of the strategic plan. Thus, the school librarian should have ways of monitoring the external environment (see External Scanning in Part II of this book) and the internal world of the school (see Internal Scanning in Part II of this book) and be thinking how these affect the strategic plan. The vision will change as the other elements of the strategic plan are altered. Although the mission may not change very much, its dynamism comes from its serving as a touchstone against which the action plans are held when they have to be reviewed as a consequence of changes in the vision. As action plans will have to be changed when the other parts are altered, they can also cause the other elements to be rewritten. Thus, the mistakes made in the design and implementation of action plans become the necessary data the planning team needs to adjust and revise. Failure is inevitable. Learning from these problems is the challenge of keeping the plan dynamic.

Understanding the Change Process

Since the implementation of an action plan is going to cause a change in one or more staff members, we should become familiar with what research tells us about this process. Although I elaborate on this dynamic in the second part of this book, we can anticipate that the people involved will resist some or all of the innovation the action plan is promoting. Luckily, there is extensive research that shows what interventions are the most effective at each step of the change process. The Concerns-Based Adoption Model is the most powerful tool to use in the educational setting. A succinct description is available at the National Academies' Web site, http://www.nationalacademies. org/rise/backg4a.htm.

Professional Development

Because overseeing the strategic plan calls for leadership skills, it would be helpful for the school librarian to be trained in the concept of leadership from the middle. Because there is growing awareness of the importance of middle managers, there has been a growing emphasis on training these essential leaders. An interesting Web site to visit is Sue Menzie's Tapestry

Leadership Concepts at http://www.tapestryleadershipconcepts.com. Particularly intriguing is her online article on "Sandwich Leadership" at http://www.tapestryleadershipconcepts.com/articles/sandwich.

Since other middle managers in a school could benefit from such training, it would be worth developing a cooperative training program with them. Since most of the issues of middle managers are unique to this "in-between" status, development of synergy should be well received. Another interesting approach is what Allan Cohen of Babson College refers to as the "Influence Model" http://www.influencewithoutauthority.com/images/Influence%20article%20 J%20Org%20Excellence.pdf. Although this is not specifically about school, he points out the value of middle managers for all organizations.

Periodic Updating

In addition to the regular monitoring and adjustment of the action plan, the greater strategic plan should be reviewed at least once per year. Although most of the sections will remain the same, continue-stop-start and current context should be visited annually. The most efficient way for these to be reviewed is to have a blog set up, within which the staff and planning team can make suggestions and comments. When the annual meeting to address the needed changes takes place, these suggestions can be reviewed. Since the school librarian(s) has the ultimate responsible for the supervision of the library program, he must decide which suggestions are mission/vision driven and which are not. It is important to point out to the staff or committee members who make the suggestions that they do or do not fit into the agreed upon strategic plan.

"Nuts and Bolts" Issues

Strategic planning is designed to be long term and mission/vision driven. It is not meant to address the bric-a-brac of daily management. Indeed, it is a process that allows us to move beyond the day-to-day concerns. This is not to say that we should not address these issues. Indeed, a school librarian would probably find himself out of work if these daily management issues were not addressed. There have been various books written on daily management of school libraries. Brief daily meetings with the entire staff are very beneficial. They should be short and highly informational. The calendar for the immediate day or two should be reviewed for anything out of the routine. Beyond that, sharing a scheduling calendar in Microsoft Outline, Google Apps, or similar programs is advised.

PART II

Participating in the strategic planning process over the last 25 years has convinced me that school librarians have unique talents to bring to a school or district planning team. In this part of the book, I will attempt to explain how the process works. Additionally, I will show how the school librarian can become a vital member of the planning team and apply strategic planning to the library program. Strategic planning by its very nature is inclusive and group oriented. A plan congruent with the whole school has an excellent chance to succeed. Once you truly enter this process, it becomes impossible to go back to business as usual. Your perspectives on schools, learning, and resources change significantly. As a school librarian, this is simultaneously a time of bewilderment and excitement. It is my hope that the excitement will come through in this explication of the process of strategic planning.

This is intended to be a guidebook for change. It is designed to stand in contrast to the typical planning that takes place in most schools. Since strategic planning will vary according to the understanding of the planning team, it is not meant to be a cookbook. Rather, it is an outline of some successful approaches within each of the major components of strategic planning. Although each phase is a stepping-stone in the process, some will receive more attention because of their relative importance. It would be presumptive for me to infer that this is the only model a team can employ. However, experience has shown that it is a successful one.

Throughout the process, I will explain the steps of strategic planning and the role of the school librarian in each. However, given the demographics of virtually all schools, the school librarian cannot hope to be successful without working with or as part of the school planning team. I will offer suggestions as to how to become an integral part of a school's planning process. Each of the elements of the plan will be explained. The responsibility of the planning team and the role of the school librarian will be presented. The desired outcome is for each school librarian to be viewed as a necessary part of the restructuring process.

This section is an outgrowth of numerous workshops I have offered throughout the country. I have been invited to present to all the major associations that involve school librarians. These and regional group offerings have allowed me to hear the comments of many school librarians and other educators. Even when the program was not a featured offering within a conference, it drew sizable numbers of participants. I hope to reach those who could not attend my workshops, and I want to afford to those who have attended the opportunity to reflect on the major elements of strategic planning. Since there is very little written on strategic planning for the school librarian, I hope this book will prove to be a catalyst for change within the profession.

As we look at the criticism directed at public education both from within and without, there appears to be consensus in a few areas. Among them is the need to produce better student outcomes, the lack of consistent national leadership, and the frequent absence of a clear vision for change on the part of the local school or school district. The last should be the first priority. A school and its school librarian cannot significantly increase student performance without developing a vision of a new, more responsive school. Only when the number of schools that have renewed themselves reaches a critical mass will national goals and direction be meaningful and attainable. Student outcomes have not and probably will not improve without a strategic planning process. Specifically, this is a process oriented toward developing a vision of how the school should evolve. Additionally, it is a systematic plan for turning that vision into reality in each school. Finally, it is totally focused on significantly improving student outcomes (scores or assessments).

When we compare long-range planning in public education to that of industry or even nonprofit organizations, education is significantly behind (Conley, 1992). This is not to say that no planning has taken place. Schools have attempted to project building space needs in a growing population and have planned to scale back in a constricting situation. We have planned for bond issues and developed elaborate bureaucracies to answer real or perceived needs. Educators have also been able to plan budgets a year or two in advance. Some pundits have called this the "Four B's" approach—buses, budgets, bricks, and butts (seating space). Factors such as powerless teachers, constrained administrators, rotating membership of boards of education, emphasis on textbooks, and curriculum coverage have tended to preserve a system that almost no one feels is adequately doing its task of preparing students for the 21st century. Enter strategic planning.

Strategic planning distinguishes itself by being not only for the long term but also visionary. It tends to focus on the big picture in the educational reform movement. It seeks to steer schools clear of interest-group pressures and reactive decision making. Strategic planning is best understood by contrasting it with typical educational planning.

What follows is an example of what usually passes for planning in schools. It will, by contrast, illustrate what strategic planning should be. In this example of nonstrategic planning, a superintendent convenes a committee of administrators and staff, including the obligatory percentage (30 to 50 percent) chosen by the bargaining unit (union). They are charged by him to come up with a state-mandated, five-year professional development plan. They are allowed release time, about five mornings, to listen to consultants and representatives of bellwether school districts. They are then asked to come up with, by brainstorming, a list of focus areas. Some 50 areas are identified. A subcommittee is appointed to condense this list into a more workable one. The new list contains 13 focus areas. At this stage, people seem to be participating and developing ownership. Planning can often experience this honeymoon period before the realities of the educational bureaucracy come to the fore.

There is a hiatus of four months after which the committee is convened for the final time. It is told by the superintendent that the 13 areas have been divided into three categories: instruction (nine), wellness (one), and incentives and rewards (three). The nine instructional areas are to be covered by requiring all staff members to take at least the introductory course to a nationally syndicated program of instructional improvement. The decision of the fit of this offering for the staffs of the schools involved is solely the superintendent's. This determination was made even though he had never taken the course himself. Both the wellness and incentives and rewards areas are relegated to study committees, which are never convened. Although the committee approves the plan, ownership is lost. When the members of the committee are questioned by their fellow faculty members as to why they voted for something they did not believe in, they say they view the process as a charade or an administrative ploy. In subsequent years, virtually no one in any of the district's schools, except committee members, can identify that there is a five-year professional growth plan. When, after five years have expired, the state department of education representative announces that she is coming to the schools to review the plan, it takes a few days to locate the document!

This plan was not strategic because it lacks many critical elements.

Specifically, if a plan is strategic, it should have each of the following elements (see figure on next page):

- External scanning (looking at our surrounding environment)

- Internal program scanning (taking a "snapshot" of our school)

- Organizational analysis (accessing our strengths and weaknesses)

- Vision and mission statements (determining what our school should look like)

- Action plans (showing how we plan to get to the vision)

By comparison to this typical approach to educational planning, strategic planning from the beginning establishes that it is ongoing, comprehensive,

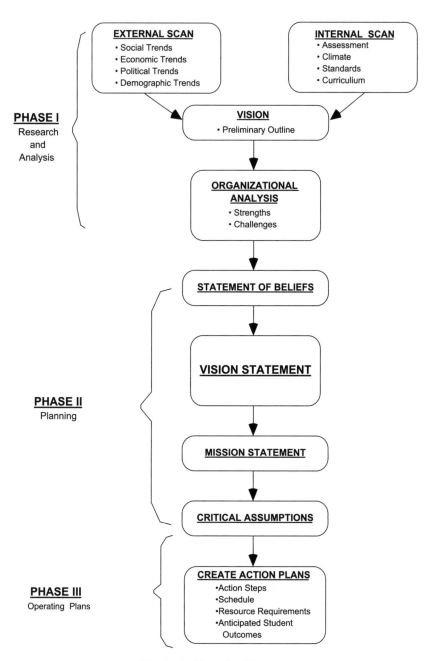

Strategic Planning Process

participatory, and systematic. One of its critical or defining elements is its use of broad questions about a school's current internal state in relation to its external environment. It attempts to deal with the unpredictability of the future (Conley, 1992). Thus, the previous example would be handled as follows:

When the individual school is asked to join the planning of a five-year professional development plan, it attempts to apprise the superintendent that it views such planning as fragmented and ultimately futile. It warns him that any change in a system, such as a school, eventually causes other changes in a ripple-effect manner (Perelman, 1988). The preferred approach is to establish a planning team to bring order to the process of educational reform. It invites the superintendent to join this planning team.

CHAPTER 12

Convening the Planning Team

There are numerous ways and means of establishing a planning team. However, the team should have certain characteristics. It should be, if possible, site based or centered in and around the reform of a single school. Although there can be assistance from the central office, the actual planning should be home grown (Fullan, 2000). It is made up of people involved in that school who see the need to change and are willing to exert the effort and donate the time to see it happen. It should be composed of those who command enough respect from their fellow staff members to endure the inevitable criticism and anger the change process brings (Leon and Davis, 2009). It should have representatives of most of the major areas and groups of the school. Although trying to get all factions represented could be a form of chaos, key elements cannot be ignored. Thus, administration, faculty, the board of education, parents, and students should be involved.

The first hurdle will probably be the selection process. We, as educators, tend to elect our representatives to committees. Although this has tended to serve us well in management-versus-labor negotiations, it is probably not the best approach to begin the change process in a school. Often the people who are elected or are appointed by the bargaining unit (union) are people who are relatively comfortable with the way the school is run. They are viewed as sturdy fighters who can stand up to management. This approach has tended to kill initiatives on the part of the agents of change in the building. Those who would promote new approaches are often viewed as different and vaguely threatening. How, then, can these midwives of change be put in a position where they can affect innovation? Before we answer this question, we should be cognizant of two other necessary components of the selection process.

Although the research is conclusive, there are indications that there are two critical elements in convening an effective planning team. The first is that the members of the team be willing to carry the standard of restructuring throughout all the ensuing battles. The second is that the team be given the support of and be nurtured by at least one influential administrator, preferably the superintendent (Fullan, 2000).

53

Let us look at an example of team selection. This will address the issues of membership, leadership, and support. In this situation, the team is convened by a principal. This follows a request by the faculty that someone oversee the dizzying array of change initiatives—assessment, cooperative learning, technology integration, process writing, reading and writing across the curriculum, critical thinking, professional development, and so on. Each of these areas is represented in the school by different committees. The committee chairs are formed into a study team called the roundtable. This appellation is chosen as being symbolic of a committee willing to share and listen on a democratic basis. The group's name will later be changed to the futures committee, reflective of the notion that there are many possible futures the school can attempt to invent for itself. The school librarian is asked to be part of this committee not because of the many reforms she is initiating in the library but because of her work on the professional development and technology committees. This points up the need for school librarians to be leaders in areas outside their usual domain. Involvement in curriculum, instruction, assessment, or literacy committees would also tend to put the school librarian in a position to be chosen as part of a planning team.

This example can be translated to schools with different governance structures (e.g., grade team leaders or skill specialists). The structure is not as important as is the perception of the need for change. Institutions usually are comfortable with the status quo. Change is difficult and usually unwelcome (O'Neil, 1993). Although part of the membership could be elected, the critical piece is that the change agents are allowed to be in an environment where the committee members are looking for better ways of doing business.

The futures committee meets three times before it begins to form its identity. Since most members play dual roles as teachers in their own disciplines and committee chairs, they immediately see the need to establish a means of planning for the future. If a method is not found, they sense that there is a high probability that discussions will deteriorate into turf battles over whose innovation should be funded. Since about half of the members are also department chairs, the scars of territorial battles are many and right below the surface. A different approach is needed, one that education systems typically do not offer (Dunsworth and Billings, 2009).

Since there few successful educational planning models, the futures committee turns to industry and nonprofit agencies. They are greatly aided by a board of education member who has many years of experience in corporate planning. He helps the committee realize from the start that its role is that of long-range planning and is not a managerial one. This is not an administrative council under a different name. His experience has told him that to mix these two functions, planning and management, causes too much confusion for everyone involved. This is a new way of thinking for schools, as is most of strategic planning.

As with most schools, the strategic planning model found in the private sector is adapted. Whereas businesses usually opt for a "top-down" approach where a planning team meets in seclusion to decide the future of the corporation, educators have made the process much more participatory (Conley, 1992).

A member of the futures committee who has had experience in municipal government realizes, after studying various approaches, that something is missing in the models or processes studied. Although most plans have a mission statement, they do not seem to embody a vision of the future. Thus, it is decided that a mission statement should not be written before a vision statement is composed. This proves to be the most important decision on the part of the committee. A mission statement should be composed after a vision is presented. Indeed, this person becomes what some researchers call the "process champion," who helps the planning team focus on the steps of the process of strategic planning. Such a person is invaluable (Conley, 1992).

At this point, the superintendent begins to attend the meetings more regularly. Although she is very busy, she is fascinated by the enthusiasm she sees coming from this mixed group. She begins to see teachers in a different light. Although they do not have her perspective or experience, they present notions of school reform that are both fresh and school based. She gives her approval for some money to be spent on substitutes so that the futures committee may meet during the school day. She also approves the principal's notion of having the home economics department cater the lunch for the committee. This and a few other perquisites help convey to the group that they have very important work to attend to. Although the business world tends to give its change agents training and amenable meeting facilities, educators are often expected to be treated as anyone else in the building and receive little attention to human comforts. Under the rubric of egalitarianism, we seem to ignore the fact that people need incentives to be able to sustain change. Individual initiative and group identity are essential parts in making strategic planning successful. Individuals tend to participate in projects such as these for one of three reasons: recognition, power, or affiliation. Those who tend to need recognition will see this as an opportunity to be valued for their contributions to the goals of the group. The members who seek power will tend to view the planning team as a source of control over the reform process. Those who desire affiliation seize on this invitation to be part of the most active and, hopefully, most respected group in the building. Simultaneously, the group must quickly develop an identity. Those who need recognition should be given tasks in each of the planning steps that make the most of their abilities. Members who want a position of authority should be shown how the process of consensus building is the road to ultimate power to change the school. Those for whom affiliation is the prime motivator should be encouraged to develop means by which the members can build an esprit de corps.

Vis-à-vis the rest of the school, all of this will cause friction from the start. If certain people are chosen to be in this special study group, others will inevitably feel left out. If the committee does not communicate what it is doing to the rest of the faculty and the greater community, it will build a wall of resentment around itself (Conley, 1992). I suspect that the only way a school can avoid having this friction becoming debilitating is by annually rotating in a sizable minority of new members. Attention has to be given to ensure that people who are dissatisfied with the status quo are in the majority. This can be accomplished by having an equal number of members elected and appointed. The appointed members should be chosen from among those people who have shown their desire to change the existing process of education.

The School Librarian and Leadership

Over the past two decades, I have been part of two national consortia sponsored by the Association for Supervision and Curriculum Development: the High School Futures Consortium and the Restructuring Consortium. Both dealt with ways of inventing the type of schools we will need. The Futures Consortium focused on what the high school of the future should look like. Since virtually every type of high school was represented, common understandings of teaching, curriculum, governance, and technology were emphasized. The Restructuring Consortium had representative schools from a variety of school systems and from across grade levels. In all, 45 schools were represented by approximately 300 educators and parents. Only a handful of school librarians were chosen to represent their schools. When the administrators of the various schools were asked why they had omitted school librarians from their planning teams, they typically replied that they did not think to include them.

One of the reasons researcher Patricia Cox mentioned as to why the school librarians seem to be the nonpersons of the educational world is the attitude of teachers and administrators toward them. She surveyed these groups as to why school librarians were not more visible. She found that they were viewed as people who have little adult-to-adult contact with other educational professionals in the building. Unless teachers or administrators can observe all the varied tasks of the school librarian over a long time frame, most see them as being less than real teachers. Although we entered this profession to help children and most of us receive our greatest satisfaction from that interaction, we now need to assume roles that include more adult interaction. It is a simple but painful fact that those who are not seen as valuable will increasingly be seen as being expendable.

The initial task for the school librarian is to make sure he is part of the local planning team. This will not be done on the strength of running an exemplary library program alone. Rather, it will come pursuant to the school librarian meeting with like-minded change agents in the school. This collaboration should occur on a common ground. The natural areas would be committee involvement with literacy, professional development, or technology. However, instructional improvement or assessment offer possibilities for synergy. We cannot afford to keep a low profile.

One of the first paradigm shifts is to begin to expand our notion of a leader in the educational community. Many of us still view this as an either/or situation. Specifically, you are either an administrator/leader or a teacher/follower. Restructuring will cause a change in the designation of leadership roles. We are beginning to see the creation of task-specific or situational leaders. These are teachers who, while remaining essentially in the classroom, assume part-time leadership roles. They could include, among others, literacy coach, writing specialist, learning specialist, instructional peer counselor, and study group facilitator (Zmuda and Harada, 2008). Since few schools can afford to hire multiple consultants to bring about needed changes, people already on staff will have to assume specific roles. The school librarian has strengths that should be capitalized on by a restructuring school. The school librarian is the closest person a school has to an information specialist. Any organization that hopes to stay current must have a person who knows how to organize information and how to access it. In addition, he has to know how reliable the source is and the characteristics of the clients of the information. Since we are always accessing information, many times we forget that not all people are as facile in this area as we are. In many respects, education is an information-poor domain (Banathy, 1991). Local decisions are often based on outdated or poorly researched information. Administrators are often satisfied with their staffs being knowledgeable in their various disciplines or grade levels. However, those disciplines or grade levels will never truly be integrated until the teaching staffs understand how everything fits together. Interdisciplinary education forces all parties to take information from various areas and turn it into a meaningful whole. The school librarian is an essential part of this synthesis. However, this integration cannot take place until the school has a plan for doing it. To be successful, a strategic plan must be driven by accurate and timely information. If not, we will have tens of thousands of schools attempting to restructure without benefit of comparative information. A school librarian is an invaluable aid in the process of networking with other schools to learn about reform and benefit from others' mistakes.

Congruence Between Plans

The school librarian is responsible for writing two strategic plans. As mentioned earlier, the school librarian is an integral part of the school's planning process and, therefore, has a responsibility to see that the plan is written and acted upon. In addition, the school librarian writes a plan for the library. Indeed, the library plan is one of many submitted by the various departments or grade levels of the school. The elements of these plans will be described throughout this part of the book. It is critical that they be written with a sense of unity or congruence in mind. Even in site-based management, a balance must always be struck between the necessary autonomy of various departments or areas and the central planning process of the school (Fullan, 1993). A plan written for the library by the school librarian will be composed for a greater audience than the school librarian. The planning team and all other parties need to be able to recognize a centrality of vision. The most eloquent plan written in isolation may even bring the program national recognition, but it is ultimately an exercise in futility if the administration and staff of the entire school do not understand and appreciate it.

What I am proposing is not going to be simple or quick. We all have to learn how to play under new rules. Maybe it would be helpful to take a notion from industry. When you take a product and add something to it through a certain process, you call it value-added manufacturing. We, as educators, tend to recoil at the notion of being compared to the makers of goods. However, we can still borrow from that world. How would a school librarian or any educator answer the question,

"What value does your program add for the student during his tenure at your school?" The related question is, "How do you measure that value?" If we hide behind platitudes and excuses rather than answer these challenges, someone else will answer them for us. Since benevolence will not reign in public education over the upcoming years, can we afford to let someone else determine our worth? Strategic planning involves a means of bringing the school librarian into a central role in answering the aforementioned challenges to the school and the library. When they are properly answered, a vision will have been developed, a vision for a restructured school and library.

There is a process to strategic planning. It has certain elements or steps: an external scan, an internal scan, an organizational analysis, a vision statement, a mission statement, and action plans.

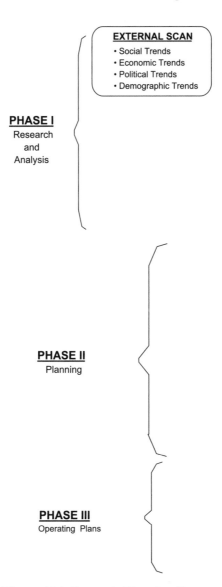

EXTERNAL SCAN
• Social Trends
• Economic Trends
• Political Trends
• Demographic Trends

PHASE I
Research
and
Analysis

PHASE II
Planning

PHASE III
Operating Plans

Figure 12.1. Strategic Planning Process

It is important to go through each step to have a successful experience (see Figure 12.1). However, it does not end there. Strategic planning should be ongoing and systematic. The school should continue to review and refine each step indefinitely. A static or nonstrategic plan is considered done when it reaches its written form. A strategic plan is never finished.

CHAPTER 13

External Scanning

As the term implies, an external scan is the process of looking out at the external environment of the school to glean the most important trends that will probably have an impact on it. Let us consider an analogy. Suppose we are entered in a sailboat race from Newport, Rhode Island, to Bermuda. We set our course based on knowledge of the external world. This should include knowledge of typical weather conditions for the time of year and of severe weather conditions. Suppose, further, that when we embark on this race we are blown off course during a storm. Any good sailor knows that the original plan will have to be altered. The external world changes, and a dynamic plan responds. This adjustment is logical and second nature to a respectable navigator. However, many educational plans are not dynamic. They are rigid to the point that if applied to this analogy, they would cause the sailor to sail back to his original course rather than set a new one. In other words, once put in print they become impervious to changes in the surrounding environment. Static plans are the norm in the educational world. We write a five-year technology plan with no built-in adjustment mechanism. However, once the strategic planning process begins, it never ends. The time and care spent on completing and understanding each step in the beginning are well worth it. You will become, as a school librarian, an invaluable resource for your school in effecting a strategic plan.

For purposes of understanding, the external world is divided into concentric circles radiating from the center (the school) but excluding it. The closest circle is the local community, which for our purposes is the local school district. Moving out to the other circles we find the state, nation, and finally the world. The inner circle, the school, will be treated in the internal scanning stage. When we execute this first step of planning, our task is to identify the trends that are emerging within these areas or circles. The typical reaction from educators at this point is to ask why it is necessary to look at the outside world. We educators are used to functioning in an information-poor environment (Joyce, Wolf, and Calhoun, 1993, 22). How is this relevant to the task at hand? The reasons are twofold. First, most of the changes that have come to education and remained have not come from within but from without. The history of public education in this country has been a series of mandates and fiats from local, state, and federal legislative bodies.

From compulsory attendance until the age of 16 to No Child Left Behind Act of 2001, few if any reforms came from the grass roots of the educational community. They came from those people outside the process who felt that only legislation could remedy a societal problem. These remedies were, almost invariably, imposed from above. In addition, they were placed on top of previous reforms. Since they were imposed from above, they tended to make schools more responsive to higher authorities than to their own students' needs (Hill and Bonan, 1993, p. 25).

The second reason is changes that eventually have an impact on us are usually developing long before we respond to them. Unless we want to be continually caught off guard, we should take a more proactive stance. If we spot a trend at the stage where we have enough time to prepare for it, we can develop an answer or plan to deal with it. The trick is to become adept at spotting trends and then projecting how they will have an impact on the school.

Looking at the "Worlds"

Although we could begin our scanning with any of the "worlds" influencing our school, it is usually easier to begin with the greater planet (see Figure 13.1). Selectivity is, obviously, important from the beginning. The charge of the planning team is to first look for major international trends. Next, it looks at national, state, and local trends. It then takes the trends and puts them in order of priority as to how they will affect the school. It is helpful to formulate categories to make organization easier. For instance, the trends might be organized in the following fashion:

- Societal trends (major shifts in society)

- Economic trends (global economic trends and their impact on the local economy)

- Educational trends (new knowledge of learning and instruction)

- Technological trends (new technology either directly influencing the learning process or affecting the learning community)

- Health trends (diseases and cures directly affecting children)

- Governmental trends (changes in how governments govern)

The list will vary, of course, with the type of school and its location. A school near a major airport would need to know about trends in transportation.

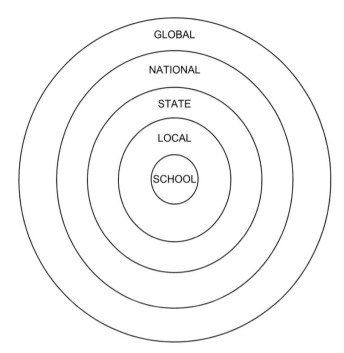

Figure 13.1. Strategic Planning Process

A technical high school would have to look at career trends on the international scene. An elementary school would need to know about developments in child care. As with all parts of strategic planning, each school will come up with a list that it feels is most appropriate to its situation. The object is to identify those specific trends that will have the greatest impact on the school (see Figure 13.2).

Although the planning team can opt to do an external scan in a short intensive session (e.g., a weekend retreat), it is usually preferable to stretch it out over a longer period. Each team member should be assigned an area (trend) to inspect. Try to assign by preference and areas of expertise. The natural tendency of team members is to question how knowledgeable educators can be in areas outside their domain (e.g., reading or science). The answer a school librarian should give is that you only have to be knowledgeable enough to find someone who is expert in that area. Often a nearby major corporation or its division will have access to global information, especially in relation to economic or demographic trends. Major utilities usually have people assigned to study trends that affect them and their customers. Health agencies are usually charged with identifying trends in the disease control area. These organizations are usually more than willing to share whatever information they have with the public. The United Way has a division in its

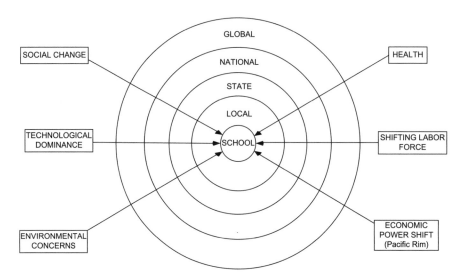

Figure 13.2. Strategic Planning Process

national headquarters that does strategic planning. This section assists local chapters with their strategic plans. Since we work with some of the same populations as the United Way, we can piggyback on some of their findings. Utility companies, especially phone companies, are constantly assessing new technologies and how they will affect different populations. Although they will withhold information that may affect their competitive stance, they will reveal the trends they have identified.

This is usually an opportune point to enlist the help of concerned parents. Often parents whose jobs give them access to information on worldwide trends do not have the time to join a planning team. However, they can help present a report on one or more trend areas. In an urban situation, municipal agencies and major public libraries can offer invaluable assistance.

It is an excellent idea to have some basic questions to be covered in each area. They should include:

- What are some of the major trends in this area?

- What impact will these trends have on the local community?

- When will these trends emerge on the local scene?

- If we could look at one or two trends per area, what would they be?

An example of trend analysis in the external scan would be to look at the rate of labor force participation by women with school-age children.

According to the Bureau of Labor Statistics, beginning in the late 1970s, more such women were working than staying home. Today, almost two-thirds of these women work. Although their percentage is smaller, a faster-growing segment is working women with children under six years old. This trend was actually quite clear to demographers over two decades ago. If strategic planning had been in effect in the early 1980s, schools might have addressed the needs of this population by planning incrementally. As a parent of children who needed child care, I would have gladly helped plan some sort of fee-based child care in the local school system. As taxpayers and voters, young parents would tend to be very supportive of a school that understands the needs of parents and preschool children. In addition, the trend in the 1980s toward more stringent academic requirements and the consequent reduction of many high school home economics courses could have been reviewed in light of the national need for safe and adequate child care. If these programs had been modified to become self-sustaining, the needs of high school students, preschoolers, and parents could have been met. Although we can attempt to meet these needs today, some 30 years after the trend was first identified, slow and gradual phase-ins are usually much less disruptive. Proactive schools can usually deal with these trends with significantly more energy and purposefulness than can reactive schools.

As an example of an external scan, what follows is Joel Barlow High School's (Redding, Connecticut) attempt to focus on the elements and events that will have the most impact on its future.

Global Issues

1. There will be a shift in economic power away from United States.
2. There will be a rise in the economic power of the Pacific Rim.
3. Emerging technology will continue to be a dominant force, especially in the areas of communications and information.
4. There will be an increased population shift toward Third World countries.
5. Although there will not be any superpower conflicts, regional conflicts and asymmetrical warfare will increase.
6. The commercial use of outer space will increase.
7. Global warming will increase.
8. With the decline of ideology, there will be a rise in economic imperialism.
9. The most dominant health issues will be epidemics, aging, and advances in biotechnology.
10. Education will be seen as increasingly important.

National Issues

1. Changes in Power Structure

    A. There will be a shift in jobs from traditional manufacturing to information/service or energy-smart manufacturing.

    B. There will be a psychological impact from being a debtor nation, especially vis-à-vis China.

    C. There will be a decline in the standard of living for most U.S. citizens.

    D. There will be a continued desire for "yuppie" things, that is, current fashions and signs of economic success.

    E. Society will become increasingly polarized between the haves and have-nots.

    F. There will be a continued fragmentation of values.

2. Technologies

    A. U.S. leadership in areas of emerging technology is threatened.

    B. The volume of information is expanding rapidly.

    C. Communications technology will steadily increase the speed of and access to information.

    D. Convenience has become a lifestyle. Businesses are catering to a society that demands convenience.

    E. Work will continue to become increasingly high tech.

    F. There will be an increased need for direct human interaction, both physical and psychological.

    G. The way people view themselves will be altered because of the dynamic tension between traditional self-sufficiency and technical dependency.

3. Population Characteristics

    A. There will be continued emigration of Third World people to America.

    B. There will be a smaller percentage of school-age children in comparison to the rest of the population, due to the aging of the baby boom generation.

    C. The conflict between cultural pluralism and assimilation will increase.

4. New World Order

    A. The economic implications of the Defense Department's restructuring of its spending patterns will have a severe impact on national and state budgets.

    B. Our volunteer army will continue.

    C. Regional conflicts will affect the availability and delivery of energy resources.

D. Developments in military technology will be transferred to consumer products.

E. The financial interdependence of the United States with other nations will become even more obvious.

F. Increased conflicts will develop more chaos in political, economic, and social spheres.

5. Space

A. It will not be used for colonization in the near future.

B. It will be used for military purposes.

C. It will be used for research and development, especially in metallurgy and pharmacology.

D. It will be used for satellite communication.

E. It will influence the development of technology throughout society.

6. Environment

A. It will increase the need for a wiser use of resources.

B. It will increase risks and economic considerations in the area of health.

C. It will cause the further development and use of resource-recovery systems.

D. It will increase the inter-town and intra-town, state, regional, and international emotional conflicts.

7. Multiple and Diverse Alliances Driven by Economic and Political Factors

A. They will simultaneously develop and restrict new markets for goods and services.

B. They will reduce or increase the availability of resources.

C. They will affect the balance of trade between the United States and other financial powers.

8. Health

A. There will be an increase in ethical considerations in the area of medical procedures, such as availability of organs for transplant and health care.

B. New health care roles will develop.

C. As costs increase, there will be a need for limits.

D. There will be an increase in the life span of most people.

9. Education

A. There will be a need to reduce the dropout rate and the number of students at risk.

B. There will be a need to increase our knowledge of international education.

    C. Reform effects will increase policy development at the regional and state levels.

    D. The availability of education will increase, mostly through the application of advanced technology, such as online learning.

Local Issues

1. Changes in the Power Structure

    A. There will be a demographic shift in the population of the town from the "native" (long-time resident) to the "technocrat" (transient with professional background and expertise).

    B. There will be a shift in political power from the old guard to the younger, active group that wants to control its families, land, schools, and tax dollars.

    C. The towns will continue to be the refuge of professionals.

    D. Established residents will try to continue as the "haves"—affluent and in political control—restricting inroads by the "have nots."

    E. This restrictive philosophy will cause a strain on the local tax base.

    F. There will be a continued willingness to let children work part time.

    G. Most parents will want social morality/values taught in schools.

    H. There will be an increased reliance on the educational system to respond to social issues.

2. Technologies

    A. Residents will continue to be employed in the technology professions.

    B. There will be an increased use of technology in schools.

    C. Schools will continue to move toward the use of "cloud" computing.

3. Population

    A. There will be an increase in the elderly population.

    B. The school-age population will gradually plateau.

    C. The socioeconomic makeup of the towns will not change, but there will be an increase in English as a Second Language families.

4. Pollution

    A. Residents are particularly vulnerable to changes in the amount and quality of natural resources.

    B. The sale of watershed lands will have an economic, political, and environmental impact on both towns.

    C. The disposal of waste will increasingly be a problem.

5. Health

A. Although there is a growing elderly population, there is not any real support for this group.

B. There is a continuing need for health services/agencies in social areas: substance abuse, pregnancy, stress, suicide.

6. Education

A. Schools will continue to be a major economic factor.

B. The majority of students will enroll in local schools.

C. There will be a small but growing percentage of students attending private schools.

D. Student preparation will continue to be toward college, specifically highly competitive ones.

E. There will be an increased reliance upon schools for social services in prevention and rehabilitation.

F. Online learning will be employed to offer more options to credit recovery or advanced placement courses.

The School Librarian as the Eyes and Ears of the Planning Team

The school librarian can and should establish a leadership position during the external scanning stage. Educators are usually unfamiliar with this type of fact finding and research. The planning team needs a person who can help people search for information in their appointed areas of investigation. The school librarian should act as a guide to the information. Among other things, he should help identify the best resources available. Since his schedule is more flexible than that of most teachers, he should offer to take return calls from agencies and help organize the information. This is an excellent time to use his collaborative skills to reinforce that he is the information specialist of the team. If he is familiar with any of the various information skills models, he can tactfully apply them to the situation. If one uses the "Big6™ Skills" approach of Eisenberg and Berkowitz, the school librarian could use it to outline the research process (Eisenberg and Berkowitz, 1990). Thus, he would ensure that:

1. The problem is defined to the satisfaction of all members.

2. An information seeking strategy is clearly defined.

3. The information is properly located.

4. A system of information extraction is in place.

5. The information is organized and presented in a way that the members can understand and use it.

6. A system of evaluating the information and how it is organized is in place.

Although some team members will have a satisfactory research scheme, most will need some help in putting together files on their area.

This is a golden opportunity to introduce the planning team to subscription databases. He can guide the members through the initial searches and then set up e-mail alerts for the various committees. He will establish his position not only as the source of valuable information but as the person who can help others become savvy in the use of information technology.

One of the habits of the mind we should be trying to promote is lifelong learning. We, as educators, should be models of this approach to learning. School librarians keep current with the changing world by helping students comprehend it. However, many educators have to be shown that they can keep abreast not only in their domains but in other areas with relative ease (Joyce, Wolf, and Calhoun, 1993). Perhaps it would be helpful to think of planning team members as our clients. It is our obligation to keep the clientele current and informed. Although they retain primary responsibility for their areas, they should come to rely upon the school librarian as someone who can help monitor major developments in those areas. This could be the beginning of an important new relationship with the faculty, administration, and community. There is no question that access to pertinent information is essential for the viability of any organization. For too long schools have not stayed current with changes in the outside world. School librarians are aware of how thoroughly the world of information has changed over the last decades. This pace of change can only increase. We should ensure that our fellow team members know how and where to access appropriate information.

Even if we do not become the chairpersons of these committees, we should become the eyes and ears of the group, the reliable source of timely and important information.

Assessing the Changing World of Libraries, Information, and Education

A school librarian has the obligation to scan the surrounding world for developments that may have an impact on the library. Begin with the greater planet and move down to the surrounding community. Major changes in the areas of communications, instruction, technology, and others have to be evaluated. Predictions as to if, how, and when they will become part of the local program should be made.

The school librarian should routinely scan as many journals, Web sites, subscription databases, and blogs that predict changes in technology and information as time and budgets permit. The American Library Association and eSchool News provide free and valuable information at their Web sites. One very obvious trend in both technology and information is the compression of information into smaller, cheaper, and more portable storage devices. Another trend is the rapid conversion to remote server storage or cloud computing. Will this trend toward cheaper and faster information access be so accelerated by wireless that school libraries will become irrelevant as storehouses of information? At the very least, we know that this trend will only increase.

The advent of Wikipedia and its clones is proving to be an interesting challenge to school librarians. We can no longer emphasize its obvious flaws and inaccuracies. It is a phenomenon that we have to account for in our information literacy instruction. For instance, recognizing that many of its articles are becoming too long and unwieldy, we can contrast them to the more concise and reading level–appropriate articles of subscription databases.

These and other trends should be assessed for their predicted impact on libraries and school librarians. Just as the world is becoming the global village that Marshall McLuhan predicted a generation ago, so the world of the school librarian is becoming a series of networks on the local, state, national, and international levels.

Before we leave the area of the external scanning, it should be noted that there appear to be some very disquieting trends. One of these has been called the "de-skilling" of the profession. Automated systems in certain libraries (university, public, and special) have caused the downgrading of functions once seen as performed by professionals, such as cataloging and reference services. Ironically, this is at a time when information specialists should be more valued than ever. This trend is forcing us to define ourselves in a different way. Looking into the future, we must find those key aspects we can bring to our schools and become the unquestioned experts in them. The subsequent steps of the strategic planning process will address how this might be done.

In summary, the external scanning phase of strategic planning is a crucial first step. The school librarian should seize upon this juncture as the place where he is viewed as being invaluable. His information-retrieval skills and organizational expertise make the school librarian indispensable in this, the introduction to the planning process. Since strategic planning is ongoing and systematic, he will continue to scan the external world for further developments. As an insider to the process, he should make every attempt at matching the information with his clientele. This role will initially be time-intensive, but the return on investment will be high. He will be viewed as an integral player on the team. Ultimately, he will be seen as the information expert of the school.

CHAPTER 14

Internal Scanning

After having looked at the outside world for trends and fixing on the ones we feel will have the greatest impact upon the school, we now must take a close look at ourselves. Probably the best way to visualize this phase is to think of it as taking a snapshot of the school. The first time you take this picture, the results may not be very clear. However, once the team learns what to focus on, the results become defined. The school becomes the subject of our lens. This is one of those times when the data the school is required to compile can be put to meaningful use. If a school has to go through an accreditation process, it usually must compile data. Also, when a school is applying for grants or awards, it is often asked to submit a profile. Federal, state, and local agencies require schools to compile records on everything from immunizations to test scores. In a high school, the guidance or student services departments are usually charged with maintaining these records. Elementary and middle schools have various ways of classifying and storing these data. Your planning team should have a member of these departments or areas. It would also be most helpful to have a member who is versed in interpreting these numbers. Administrators, guidance counselors, and mathematics teachers are familiar with numerical interpretation.

If we think of the analogy of sailing from Newport to Bermuda, this is the step where the captain inspects her craft. She looks for all the instruments she knows that she will need for the voyage. She knows that there is a competition, which causes her to see if the craft is properly fitted for the journey. She knows what her hull (maximum) speed is. She inspects her sails and rigging. She inventories her supplies. She assesses the ship's seaworthiness and ability to withstand the rigors of an ocean race. Ultimately, she judges its ability to win the race.

External and internal scanning are very closely related. External scanning tells us what the outside world is like (see Figure 14.1) and how it will affect us. Internal scanning forces us to look at ourselves to see how well prepared we are to handle the challenges of the outside world. Internal scanning is usually a difficult juncture in the planning process. It is problematic for two very important reasons. The first is that the data most schools have readily available are usually quite negative in nature. The second is that if we really invest the time and energy needed to do a worthwhile external plan, it

73

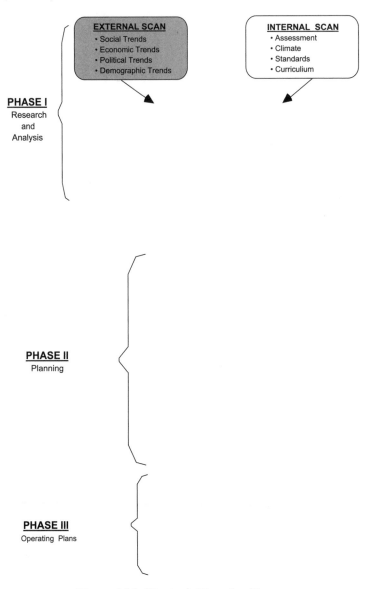

Figure 14.1. Strategic Planning Process

will become obvious where there is an appreciable gap between the needs of the future and how the school is addressing those needs. Let me address each of these issues, separately.

Because various government agencies require us to keep track of absentees, arrests, pregnancies, vaccinations, and so forth, teams are usually displeased with the first data collection effort. Even when test scores and other proficiency criteria are added, the picture is still too negative. We know, quite rightfully, we are much more than these numbers. Even if the numbers are relatively positive, they amount to little more than temperature taking. Just as the temperature tells the medical professional some significant things, so too does the initial data collection. However, a good diagnostician uses the temperature reading as one of many indicators of good health. So too must we look at these data as, perhaps, accurate but incomplete. The team must begin to develop its own assessment tools to better judge where the school is. Some schools have turned to marketing experts or polling experts who have a sense of how to elicit from various groups their perceptions of the school. Others have taken a close look at their assessment techniques and developed local measurements that are more precise. Still others have done surveys of alumni over different intervals (2, 4, and 10 years after graduation) to ascertain how the school prepared them for the next step they faced in their education or their life. As with most strategic planning, the team will have to decide what the most appropriate response to the need is. No outside expert could know the local situation better than the school team. The team can make use of the expertise of others. However, the team should choose the methods of data collection with which it feels most comfortable.

Be prepared for a certain amount of dissonance at this point. An accurate internal scan will probably show an institution that is seemingly disconnected from the trends of the outside world. The greatest corporations in the world stay great by constantly monitoring and adjusting to the outside world. Even they have been caught off guard by severe economic downturns and so-called disruptive innovations. Schools will have to develop answers to the threats such as privatization, tax rebellions, and epidemics. Lest we revert to the cynicism that has plagued education and educators, we must respond by bringing all of our resources to bear to discover how our internal world is prepared to meet the challenges from without.

Following is a list of categories of an internal scan of the same high school that was used for the external scan.

INTERNAL SCAN

    I. STUDENT POPULATION

        A. Enrollment (a narrative on the characteristics of the present student body and an enrollment projection over the next five years)

        B. Ethnic composition

        C. Language (languages spoken at home)

        D. Special education (a complete description of the program and its population)

    E. English as a Second Language

    F. Chapter I (a complete description of the program and its population)

    G. Early graduates

    H. Non-graduates

    I. Students choosing nontraditional courses (online, early college, internships, independent study)

II. STUDENTS AT RISK

    A. Retention (students kept back or needing an extra year of high school)

    B. Student fitness (results of national physical fitness exam of the incoming ninth graders administered by the physical education department)

    C. Failures and near-failures (organized by class and by student; names are not included)

    D. Attendance (average daily attendance, plus tardies and early dismissals organized by number of students and class year)

    E. Depression (cases reported by school psychologist)

    F. Drop-outs

    G. Pregnancies

    H. Child abuse

    I. Suicides (including attempts and threats)

    J. Substance abuse (survey of substance use by students and reports of the number of students being referred or counseled)

    K. Discipline (review of administration's disciplinary reports)

    L. Sexual harassment (complaints reported and action taken)

    M. Regular and frequent monitoring (other services offered through student services to track student progress)

III. STUDENT ASSESSMENT

    A. TASK test

    B. PSAT

    C. National Merit Scholarships

    D. SAT

    E. I.Q. Tests

    F. Proficiency Tests

    G. Connecticut Mastery Tests

    H. Comprehensive Testing Program (compared to suburban stanines)

    I. Student Based Assessment Program (showing attempts at alternative assessment of student progress)

    J. Lexile scores of rising ninth graders

IV. STUDENT PLANS (an analysis of the plans of various graduating classes with follow-up surveys after two years)

V. SPECIAL PROGRAMS

    A. Student activities (data concerning student activities and participation)

    B. Advanced study (the number of students in honors and advanced placement courses)

    C. Study skills (the number of students enrolled in study skills and corrective reading and writing courses)

    D. Remediation (the number of students enrolled in remedial courses or requiring the Academic Learning Center)

    E. Library use (includes number of students, range, and type of books and materials circulated or accessed online)

    F. Athletic programs (participation in athletics as broken down by class and sex)

VII. COURSE REGISTRATION (narrative description of course enrollment by department and course)

VIII. SCHOOL TIME (a comparison with neighboring towns of the number of minutes allotted to instruction, daily)

IX. FACULTY

    A. Projected retirement by the year 2015

    B. Professional development activities (a description of the professional development program and a budgetary analysis)

X. COMMUNITY PARENTAL INVOLVEMENT (a narrative describing the many connections between the community and the school)

XI. USE OF SCHOOL FACILITIES

XII. TECHNOLOGY (results of various surveys describing faculty and student use of technology)

XIII. FINANCIAL SUPPORT (an historical description of per pupil expenditures)

A thorough internal scan necessarily leads to the next phase, the organizational analysis. However, it also helps us to focus for the first time on our vision statement. The gaps or discrepancies between the external and internal scans will become the focus areas for the vision statement. The vision of our school in the future is one that addresses, as best it can, the needs of the population it serves. The vision will come from an accurate

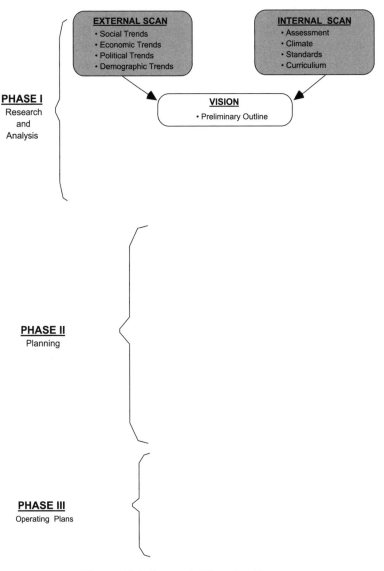

Figure 14.2. Strategic Planning Process

reading of our environment and an understanding of where we now are vis-à-vis the external scan (see Figure 14.2).

The School Librarian as Record Keeper and "Snapshot Archivist"

The planning team will need someone to help organize and disseminate the information it gathers on the internal scan. The skills of the school librarian in the areas of cataloging and collection development should be utilized. In building a Web accessible database, the school librarian can help reflect the priorities of the team. If the school maintains a professional library already, this can be seen as a complement to the resource file the team is building. The book, materials collection, and subscription databases can be groomed to reflect not only the needs of the students but the resources a planning team will need to succeed.

All materials collected should be cataloged with subject heading and categories team members recognize. As part of the proactive stance the school librarian must take, significant efforts must be taken to ensure that the team members know how to access the information within this collection. Since online cataloging allows keyword access, materials already in the collection should be tagged with words commonly used by the team (e.g., assessment, quality, impact of divorce, and so on). Most, if not all, of the information should be Web accessible. As research scientists can now scan databases for the most current findings in their areas of concern, so too should educational planners be able to find needed information from both the library and from the outside. As storage capacity of computers increases and telecommunications costs decrease, it will be important to help each team member build a powerful database that reflects his information needs.

The benefits of taking such an approach are many. Among the most obvious is that the team will have the current and vital information it needs to make the best decisions. Another is that the school librarian will be viewed as the person who helped design this information system. Wikis, blogs, and shared documents should be very helpful at this stage of the planning process. If current and appropriate information is valued by the team, so too will the school librarian be valued. Since each team will collect different sets of materials, it is essential that the school librarian know the contents of the "collections" and how to access them. As strategic planning matures, team members will inquire who said what at a certain conference or workshop. In addition, new members will have the benefit of past experiences in dealing with certain issues. The value of the school librarian to the planning team in these situations would be difficult to overstate. He is always developing an archive of the different "snapshots" the team has taken. As time goes on, he will be responsible for keeping the corporate memory for the team.

The School Library's Report Card

We must take a snapshot of the library in developing our strategic plan. An internal scan of the library should incorporate whatever it takes to present an accurate picture of the library and its program. Just as the first attempt at capturing the school in a snapshot will seem inadequate, so too will it be difficult to reflect the totality of the library's program.

We can begin with the data most readily available, usage statistics. If we keep attendance logs, we can at least know how many students and teachers use the facility. If these statistics are compiled annually, we can get a sense of whether these records reveal trends. Statistics can also be used to do a "market analysis" of the collection. Most of the circulation management computer programs have statistics programs in them. These statistics packages allow us to see which parts (Dewey ranges) of the collection are most heavily used. Some are so specific that we can "zoom in" on the part of the collection that appears to be getting the most attention. When we are done, we should have a list of areas within the collection that deserve the most attention when purchasing books and materials. Most subscription databases also have statistical packages built into them. Although we do not get the topical breakdown we would with a circulation program, we can get a sense of how often a subscription database is used and what specific product is the most popular. If we combine these three areas (attendance, circulation, and database use), we can begin to get a sense of how the library is used and what trends are developing. This can be seen as our initial assessment or report card. Additionally, it can be used locally, statewide, and nationally to compare and assess library programs (Rogers, 1993).

Although we tend to use quantitative data to do our initial scan, we will want to look beyond the numbers and begin to look at the quality of the program. There are a number of ways to capture more than numbers. We can conduct surveys of our clients. The faculty and administration is an excellent place to begin. Faculty and administration surveys can be composed by the school librarian using designs such as those suggested in David Loertscher's *Taxonomies of the School Library Media Program* (2000). Rather than straight opinion surveys, these designs would tell us how we are perceived by those who use the library the most vis-à-vis those who do not use it much. This can help us design outreach programs that will be more than general public relations.

We can take the same approach with students. Loertscher's *Taxonomies* suggests ways of discovering student attitudes and perceptions of the library. As our primary clientele, we must know how they view the program and how they might be representing it to their parents. The finest collection available is practically worthless if our clients do not know what it contains and how to access it. We cannot know to which population to direct our outreach if we do not identify it.

Probably the most helpful population in the self-evaluation of the library is our recent alumni. If we can survey them according to how we prepared them for the library or information needs of the next phase of their education, we can collect data that will have a high priority when we are analyzing the effectiveness of our program. Students tend to be very responsive to this type of survey, especially if it is conducted by the school librarian, either face-to-face or via e-mail. The school librarian is acknowledging that he values their opinions in a vital area. The surveys do not have to be longer than five or six questions. You can usually organize the answers more quickly by conducting the questioning in a semi-structured way. Thus, try to ask the most important question or two in the beginning and follow the interviewees where they want to go. If you carry a notebook, you can find a few opportunities during the year to discuss the library's program with recent graduates. After conducting a number of these impromptu surveys, it will become clearer how to draw out the information you need to evaluate your program. A sample of these questions follows:

1. Do you have to do any research? If yes,

2. What are some of your greatest difficulties?

3. Who do you turn to when you need assistance with research?

4. Where do you do most of your research?

5. Do you ever use the Joel Barlow High School subscription databases?

6. What could we have done to make this process easier for you?

7. Do you have any other suggestions?

If you are working at a school that must periodically go through the accreditation process, there is a section on the library. Although the questions or indicators may not be as focused as one would wish, they can give the school librarian a sense of how the library is viewed. It behooves us to see that these surveys reflect the type of program we feel is vital in an information age. If we feel that they reflect the library programming of 10 or 20 years ago, we should make this known to the accrediting agency. If we do not monitor and adjust the way we are evaluated, someone else will.

Finally, the snapshot we present of the library will probably cause a sense of disquiet. After comparing it to the external scan, we will know that the library of a year or so henceforth will have to be different than what we find today. We did not invent the world of rapid change, but if we do not respond to it, we will eventually be seen as no longer vital to educating youth. If we are the part of the school most closely associated with information, we have to recognize that information and its delivery are changing at a dazzling rate. The next steps of strategic planning, organizational analysis, vision and mission statements, and action plans, are the means to address the dissonance caused by comparing the external and internal scans.

CHAPTER 15

Organizational Analysis

If we have done a proper job, the external and internal scans will help us analyze the strengths and weaknesses of our school. Thus, the planning team now begins an analysis or evaluation. This must precede any description of how the school might be restructured (see Figure 15.1). The eventual vision statement will be based on the data of the external and internal scans and the evaluations of the organizational analysis.

In many respects, this is the simplest phase of the strategic planning process. First, the planning team must identify the categories for organizing the analysis. These should include instruction, curriculum, technology, community involvement, school climate, professional development, and governance (administration). The first three are directly connected to student outcomes (Joyce, Wolf, and Calhoun, 1993) and the last two support innovation. There should be an attempt to list the strengths and challenges (weaknesses) of each. Although not every category will have both, most will.

Using the analogy of the Newport to Bermuda race, this would be the phase where the captain ascertains the ship's and crew's strengths and weaknesses. This is most valuable and accurate after doing an external and internal scan. She must know the external world in which she will sail. She must know what her craft and crew is capable of in this environment. The comparison of the two, the external and internal environments, enables the captain to come up with a list of strengths and weaknesses. If she is a good captain, she does all in her power to see that the weaknesses are corrected without compromising the strengths. Knowing that she wants to win the race, she must appraise the ability of the ship to sail at racing speeds as well as its seaworthiness. Part of her list is going to be responsive to the external scan, specifically the average wave height and prevailing winds. The other part of the list is determined by the fitness of the craft and the crew. Since she cannot change the former, she must adjust the latter according to the resources available. Finally, the priority order of the list is determined by availability of funds, feasibility, and time considerations.

Let us look at the category of curriculum as an example of organizational analysis. On the strengths side, we might identify that our school has a diversified curriculum, taught by experienced professionals. We might further identify that we have the financial support to update and that we have been

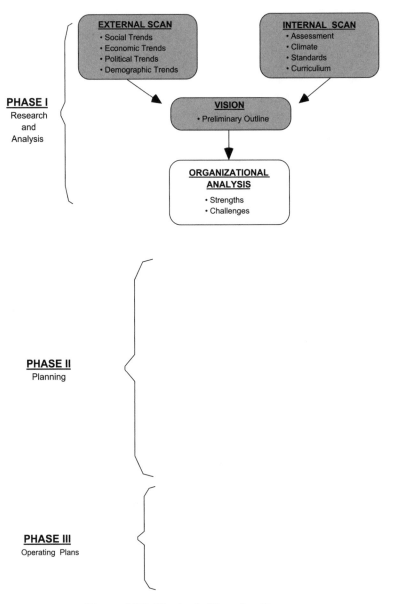

Figure 15.1. Strategic Planning Process

generally successful in preparing our students for the next phase of their education. Finally, we perceive that we have strong traditional content within the curriculum areas.

On the challenges side, we note that we do not truly have a core curriculum—systematic instruction in thinking, writing, speaking, reading, and research—in place. There appears to be little emphasis on resource-based learning. Further, we could identify that there is no systematic approach for promoting interdisciplinary studies.

Focus Groups

Since the organizational analysis is the step preceding the most crucial phase, the development of the vision statement, it is essential to involve as much of the faculty and community as possible. Although some faculties are small enough to be brought into the planning process as a group, there are other ways to get the input of larger groups. A survey may be designed to see if the faculty agrees with the planning team's notion of strengths and challenges. This is an opportune time to open up a dialogue between the team and the rest of the faculty. The survey could be developed by an ad hoc committee composed of team and non-team members. It could then be presented at a faculty meeting. This would be an appropriate time to present the findings of the internal and external scans. The faculty should be given time to ponder the survey and return it to the survey committee. To further involve the faculty, the results of the survey could be turned over to focus or testing groups. Borrowing from marketing techniques, these groups should be made up of people who will "use the product." Thus, if we want to develop a vision statement that most of the faculty, administration, and community will support, representatives of those populations should be in the focus groups. Although it is advisable to have a member of the planning team available to each focus group to explain the results of the external and internal scans, the focus groups must come to their own conclusions as to the strengths of and challenges to the school.

The reasons for transferring decision making to these focus groups are many. It is an excellent way to open the planning process to the greater community. It gives the planning team a more accurate reading of how the wider community will respond to the eventual strategic plan. It can help to find errors that the planning team is blind to. Finally, it is a good way to groom potential members for the planning team.

Each of the focus groups should have an opportunity to present its findings to the entire faculty or greater community. Although there can be as many focus groups as there are volunteers to fill them, it is not advisable to have more than three or four. Each should consist of no more than five members plus the planning team representative. Each focus group should present its perspective on what the strengths and challenges are. If these groups can independently present their findings to the whole faculty, there is a greater opportunity for debate and fermentation of ideas. This could happen through a live meeting, a wiki, or a blog. Every opportunity should be taken to discover how the faculty, administration, and community are responding to the findings. If there is a feeling of resentment toward the planning team for being elitist, this is the juncture at which those feelings can be addressed. If the planning team were to develop the list of strengths and challenges on its own, it would be very vulnerable to accusations of not being interested in faculty participation. Although some critics of this process will find this to be cumbersome and time consuming, most educators will realize that this is a good faith attempt at bringing in as many voices as possible to the decision-making process.

Once the voice of the people (faculty, administration, and community) is heard, either through a wiki, blog, survey, or face-to-face discussions, a list of strengths and challenges is compiled. There should be an attempt to put this list in priority order. Once this is done so a vision of what the school should become will be clearer. Since the dissonance felt at comparing the external scanning and internal scanning results is the true beginning of the vision development, we are now ready to write the vision statement.

This is an example of an organizational analysis using the previously mentioned categories. It was used as part of the planning process at Joel Barlow High School.

INSTRUCTION

Strengths

- Experienced staff
- Attention is given to thinking, writing, problem solving
- High academic standards
- Many levels of instruction
- Student-centered classroom activities in some areas

Challenges

- To make effective use of available teacher time
- To increase access to and distribute information on instruction
- To use assessment results
- To systematically monitor trends and ongoing research of important issues affecting education
- To understand the nature of student involvement in the learning process
- To enhance higher-order thinking skills
- To improve student writing
- To establish more interdisciplinary relations

CURRICULUM

Strengths

- Diversified curriculum
- Expertise of faculty
- Successful preparation of students for college
- Strong traditional content

Challenges

- To develop an effective core curriculum
- To promote interdisciplinary relations

TECHNOLOGY

Strengths

- Increased use of technology
- School plant and facility

Challenges

- To use new and developing technology, especially computer networks, to expand opportunities for learning by students and staff
- To provide needed computer hardware/software
- To train faculty and staff to use the technology

COMMUNITY INVOLVEMENT

Strengths

- Support from parents and board of education
- Financial support for updating curriculum

Challenges

- To use the mass media to provide more information about JBHS
- To establish a community service internship for curriculum and extra-curricular activities
- To develop a community resource bank

SCHOOL CLIMATE

Strengths

- Supportive environment for all members of the school
- High use of the library
- Use of collaborative learning concepts

- Reasonable class size
- High attendance rate (staff and students)

Challenges

- To promote a sense of belonging for some students
- To develop more collegiality
- To help teachers become researchers

PROFESSIONAL DEVELOPMENT

Strengths

- Abundant staff development opportunities

Challenges

- To coordinate professional improvement to meet student needs

GOVERNANCE

Strengths

- Teachers' advisory committee
- Strategic planning commitment
- Supportive administration

Challenges

- To define roles more clearly
- To increase teacher involvement in decision making

The School Librarian and the Organizational Analysis

Throughout the external scanning process, the school librarian should point out to the planning team how the world of information is rapidly changing. During the internal scan, the school librarian should note how schools are usually behind industry in adjusting to changes in information delivery and retrieval. The organizational analysis stage is the opportunity to show how the school is outdated as an information system. In relying so heavily on textbooks and teacher knowledge as the font of information for the students, the school cannot hope to keep up with the dizzying changes in the world around it. If we want to promote lifelong learning so that our students can adjust to the myriad of changes they will encounter, the present model for learning has to change. Since the planning team has just gone through the process of learning about the outside world so as best to plan for the future, the school librarian can use this as an opportunity to emphasize that learning should always involve some elements of external scanning. All subjects, even mathematics, are changing so rapidly that we can no longer ignore these changes' impact on instruction. Regardless of the level, teachers and students must be made comfortable with the changes around them. The school librarian sees many of these changes first. Since the school librarian is not locked into a text or curriculum, her adjustment to new information is much easier than that of the traditional classroom teacher. In many respects, the school librarian is the model of the teacher of the future. Her source of information is constantly being updated, her approach to instruction is more inductive than deductive, and her outlook is interdisciplinary and global (Zmuda and Harada, 2008). If the school librarian can effectively communicate these aspects to the planning team and the faculty, the library should appear on the strengths side of the list and the present information delivery system on the challenges side.

Looking at the School Library Through the Eyes of Others

During the organizational analysis stage, we have to compile a list of strengths and challenges for the library. The initial list should be drawn up by the school librarian(s) involved. However, it is vital to discover how others see the program. Taking the data compiled during the internal scan, we can see how our clientele views us. There should also be evaluations of the library by the administration. If that is possible, the school librarian should help develop the survey being used by the focus groups. It should contain questions about attitudes toward and frequency of use of the library. Although we will see many of the strengths we had already identified, there will be some we did not think to mention. Also, there will be challenges we did not anticipate. If we want the library to be an integral part of the restructured school, we must be aware of the perceptions of our constituents. This calls for more than a little bit of courage. Most substantive change involves risk taking, and this is no exception. Once the list of strengths and challenges for the library has been finalized, a vision should be relatively easy to develop. If the list has too many strengths vis-à-vis challenges, you probably have not done a thorough enough organizational analysis. The library of the future will be different because education and the world of information will be evolving into something other than what we now know. If one reads *Honda: An American Success Story,* it is difficult to forget Honda's response to winning "Car of the Year" for its Accord. Instead of producing basically the same automobile the following year, it radically changed the design. Although it was proud of its accomplishment, it realized that it won the designation by adapting to the changing world of automobile technology and government regulation (Shook, 1988). Not surprisingly, it continues to garner the highest awards for its new Accords and Acuras. Even for nationally recognized school library programs, to stay the same is to fall behind.

If the library program has very few strengths as compared to challenges, the charge is to come up with a vision radically different from what now exists.

CHAPTER 16

Vision Statement

The development of the vision statement is the most vital stage of strategic planning. The prior stages are the preparation for writing it. The statement is an educated projection of how the school will change in the next three to five years. It forecasts the school's response to its changing environment. It is based on a realistic portrait of the school. It is derived from a consensus of all parties involved. It should be both realistic and inspirational. It should be specific enough that someone could, five years hence, assess whether the school has moved toward the vision or remained stagnant. However, it cannot be so detailed as to hamper the change process when new information comes along. It is more than a philosophy and objectives statement, although the philosophy of the school should be evident in it. It should reflect the most important findings of the internal and external scans as well as the organizational analysis (see Figure 16.1). It should be revised according to the wishes of the greater community. If these elements are present, the vision will also be unique (Curran, 1991). Finally, it should be viewed as a living document, in need of revision in response to changes in the external and internal worlds (Curran, 1991).

Let me invoke the sailing analogy here to explain the vision statement stage. Imagine that we are sailing to a destination about which we know very little. Indeed, the farther from home port we get, the less we know. Thus, in contrast to the Newport to Bermuda analogy, the destination is not known. No one before has sailed this exact route. Perhaps it would be instructive to look at the experience of Christopher Columbus. Although history does not record him as a great humanitarian or effective governor, he is indisputably one of the great visionaries of all time.

In reading Samuel Eliot Morrison's *Admiral of the Ocean Sea: A Life of Christopher Columbus.* one discovers a navigator of extraordinary abilities and insight. Although self-taught, Columbus could read the Latin scientific tracts of his era. His external scanning told him that reigning scientific theories, all of which were based on Ptolemy's calculations, inaccurately measured the earth's circumference. A physician from his native Genoa had calculated that Cathay (China) and an island off its coast (Japan) could be reached by means of a western route. After doing an internal scan of his resources and abilities, he presented the results of his organizational analysis to Queen Isabella of Spain. At first, she rejected his proposal. It was only

91

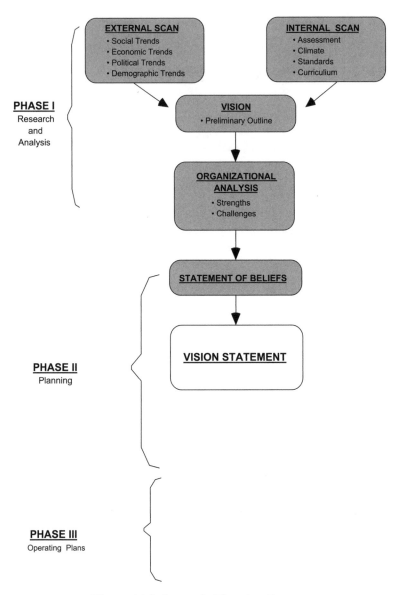

Figure 16.1. Strategic Planning Process

after the second time, when he presented a more vivid picture or vision, that she took the risk of supporting him. Las Casas, one of the diarists of Isabella's court, described his presentation: "When he had made up his mind, he was as sure he would discover what he did discover, and find what he did find, as if he held it in a chamber under lock and key" (Morrison, 1942).

Columbus retained his vision during his voyages. Although he died believing he had found the western outpost of the Orient, he adjusted his vision through a total of four voyages. By keeping a detailed log and by showing extraordinary navigational and leadership skills, he would change the course of history. His vision was altered as his environment changed and resources increased or diminished. What he wound up with was not what he initially envisioned, but his vision was the reason he discovered what he did. Although he was not a rigid slave to his vision, it was what motivated him. As his environment changed, so too did his vision. This is what is meant when describing a vision statement as a living document.

When we write a vision statement for a school, we are attempting to articulate where our school is headed. It is a scenario that describes the future we wish to see. The vision statement is designed to reflect the philosophy and objectives of the school and, at the same time, acknowledge the impact of the larger society.

In describing the future, it is not wise to project over more than five years. Indeed, the closer to the present, the more detailed we can be. This forces us to be accountable for what we will do in the near future. At the same time, it allows us to project where we feel these developments will take us.

The vision statement should have sections reflecting each part of the external and internal scans. Thus, there should be acknowledgments of those trends in the global, national, state, and local scene that will have the greatest impact on the school. In presenting how the school is expected to change, emphasis should be placed on those elements of the organizational analysis that were identified as being challenges. Finally, the nature of these changes should be specific to the categories investigated. Thus, they should include sections on the following: curriculum, the role of the student, assessment of student outcomes, the teacher's role, technology, instructional strategies, school governance, and organization. The statement should leave no doubt as to which direction the school is moving, and what it will probably look like in the process. As strategic planners, we are asked to set sail for a destination we do not know, a world we must predict. We will shape and reshape that vision as we journey (Fullan, 2000).

What follows is an example of a school's vision statement. Since it was developed by Joel Barlow High School, it was derived from the earlier cited external scan, internal scan, and organizational analysis.

Vision Statement for Joel Barlow High School

The creation of a vision is an essential component of the planning process. The vision statement is a scenario that describes the future we expect to see.

The context is that of global, state, and local conditions, as extrapolated from current trends. The vision for the institution is designed to reflect the philosophy and objectives adopted by the school community and at the same time acknowledge the impact of the larger society.

Global

The fast-breaking events now transforming social, economic, and political conditions throughout the world caution us to be tentative in our attempt to create a global vision. The only certainty is that when our students reach adulthood, the world will be very different from the one they know today.

Increasingly powerful technology will bring both the benefits and challenges of instant, far-reaching communication. Divisions will intensify between those nations and people who achieve power and prosperity in this high-tech world and those who are less advantaged, burdened by ignorance and poverty. Forces for international cooperation and unification will compete with rising demands for tribal and ethnic recognition and status. Environmental pollution will be a continual concern.

National

Within the United States, expanding needs for services in competition with growing resistance to taxation will continue to create dilemmas for policy makers. The demands of an economy based on high technology, coupled with inequities in education and employment, will hasten the trend toward cultural and economic polarization. The demand for a unified community approach to the provision of social services will force schools to work closely with, if not be subsumed by, human services programs.

Dissatisfaction with the schools and with student performance in international competition will foment efforts toward restructuring the governance and financing of the educational system. Curriculum reforms proposed by professional organizations, government agencies, and other interest groups will compete for attention and funding. Voucher plans, state and national tests, business/school coalitions, foundation support for public education, regional magnet schools, residential high schools for gifted and talented students, site-based management, and a plethora of other proposals will have their proponents.

State

In comparison to the rest of the nation, Connecticut finds itself to be very well educated and wealthy, but also very old. The present economic downturn has caused the state government to tap a funding source (tax base) more equitable than sales or property taxes. This conflict should increase as the competition for dollars to fund education and human services increases.

The demographic trends show a proportionally smaller population under age 21 and a greater percent of the population over 75. With the meteoric rise in medical costs, this older population will need more state funds. Since more people will be helping to support elderly parents and a smaller proportion will have school-age children, there will be a need to present support of education as a civic responsibility and not just a parental duty. Some of the needs of both populations might be met with innovative programs and use of school buildings.

With the growing pressure from the federal government and such high expectations on the part of adults, Connecticut must come up with a way to ensure that every child succeeds. With a fifth of its children born out of wedlock, a tenth of all youth below the poverty line and a middle class seemingly unwilling to raise taxes, the next decade would appear to be tumultuous. Efforts to reduce inequities through desegregation plans or restructuring of school districts will have an impact.

Local

The schools will continue to be a major social and cultural force. The majority of the school-age population will be enrolled in local schools. Parents will continue to demand rigorous and competitive academic preparation for their children, with considerable attention paid to individual needs. Technology will be accepted and expected.

There will be a growing need to coordinate the schools in the areas of curriculum and skills.

In addition to academic training, the schools increasingly will be relied on to provide health and social services in prevention and rehabilitation and to teach moral and ethical values. At the same time, resistance to school spending can be expected to grow, a consequence of general economic conditions, the declining percentage of households with children, and the changes in state finances and support.

Institutional

The societal forces for change outlined previously can be expected to have a significant effect on the organization and operation of Joel Barlow High School. To reconcile conflicts within the community, greater efforts will be made to communicate information and to ascertain public opinion concerning the goals and purposes of the school.

Programs for adults and alternative programs for students will be offered regularly. These will include access to courses, evening programs, and services from the library to day care. To meet the increasing demands of various constituencies, more time must be allowed for student instruction and activities and for staff training. This need will be met by a change in the calendar, in the daily schedule, and in the assignments of teachers. There will be pressures to increase the number of school days and lengthen the school day.

In addition to revision in organization and services, specific changes can be expected in curriculum, in the roles of students and teachers, in the use of technology, and in methods of instruction and assessment.

Curriculum

Curriculum content will become increasingly integrated, although individual disciplines will continue to maintain their unique perspectives and methods of inquiry. The organizing principle will be real-life situations and the larger social context. The content will include a variety of cultures and viewpoints. Community service and cultural diversity will be important components.

Transferable and marketable skills such as reasoning, problem solving, communication, and collaboration will be emphasized. Fine and practical arts will continue to be important. Students will become aware of their own thinking processes and styles of learning. The goal will be to provide students with learning strategies that will prepare them for change and for a lifetime of mental and physical fitness.

Student Role

Students will become increasingly responsible for their own learning and growth. They will learn to set realistic goals, to value themselves and others, and to develop social and interpersonal skills.

They will be expected to practice, observe, participate, listen, ask questions, volunteer, cooperate, decide, create, revise, perform, attend to criticism, inspire, and appreciate.

They will do actual research, gather information from various content areas, and understand why what they learn is true (or false).

They will become confident in their ability to apply knowledge, solve problems, make meaning of and link elements of content, make and test conjectures, discuss issues, and communicate orally, visually, and through the written word.

Teacher Role

The teacher will continue to design and provide instruction, create a variety of strategies for learning, organize materials and equipment, stimulate interest, guide, encourage, foster appreciation, oversee growth, and diagnose and assess performance.

In addition the teacher will be a model and facilitator for students, working with them individually and in groups. The teacher will draw on experience and expertise to illustrate and illuminate the beauty, utility, and enjoyment of the field of study, and will be a co-learner, exploring issues and problems with students and sharing in research efforts.

The teacher will stay current in the discipline, continue to develop professionally, collaborate with business and industry, act as a resource for other departments, participate in interdisciplinary teams, and collaborate on curriculum development.

Technology

Technology will gain in use as a powerful tool for the enhancement of learning in every discipline. As new and more powerful technologies replace time-consuming and difficult mechanical operations, the students will gain freedom and power. They will see that learning is more than memorizing and that frequently the question is more important than the answer.

As more and more information becomes available via technology, students will need to learn how to evaluate it quickly and determine what is useful.

In music, the computer will be used to compose without the difficulties of the mechanics of writing. With the power to reproduce the sound of any instrument, the student will hear the full orchestration of his composition. The computer will also be used to simulate recording studio techniques and to help students to learn aural skills, music theory, and music history.

The computer will be used in art through a computer art/graphics tie-in. In desktop publishing, for example, students will explore how the image of graphics and words affects meaning. Thanks to editing programs such as Photoshop and iPhoto, photography instruction will be radically changed.

In mathematics, the computer will reduce the need for paper-and-pencil arithmetic and give power to students to discover concepts, make and verify conjectures, and do mathematics not possible before.

In science, students will use the computer for collecting and graphing data, simulations, and drill and practice. They will become familiar with new technologies such as the scientific search engine WolframAlpha.

An important use of the computer in many disciplines is for the location and gathering of information. In the library, the development of programs such as Google Scholar, Java-based search engines, and artificial intelligence will accelerate the pace of change to multimedia and interactive environment. There will be a movement from textbook orientation to a condition where, through a process of instantaneous information retrieval, students and teachers become discriminating consumers of a wealth of data.

Broadband internal connections will link Joel Barlow with other high schools. With desegregation, we may see regional centers instead of school districts where interactive technology replaces traditional classroom instruction.

Increasingly, the computer will be used for remediation, test-taking practice, analytical skills, composing, reading speed and comprehension, and vocabulary development in English and foreign languages.

Administrative and guidance department applications of technology will increase as well. Student management programs will promote the data management of instructional improvement.

Instructional Strategies

Students will work in a variety of settings. Attention will be given to methods of increasing student participation and engagement, with sensitivity to age, development needs, and learning styles. Where appropriate, classes will be of mixed abilities, supported by technology.

Students will be engaged in process writing, role playing, independent research, simulations, hands-on activities, and discussions. In all disciplines, there will be a move toward cooperative learning groups, with students working together to solve real-life problems.

Specialized facilities such as the Writing Resource Room, computer labs, and learning centers will be widely used.

Assessment

Assessment will be used for identification, diagnosis, remediation, recognition of achievement, and evaluation of the program.

Writing and problem-solving assignments, creative projects, and performances will measure levels of accomplishment. Students will be assessed on their level of knowledge and their skills in research, problem solving, collaboration, and communication, including listening. Student portfolios will be kept to examine progress over several years.

In addition to general skills, each area of study will have established criteria and standards of performance related to the discipline. Students will increasingly establish their own goals and expected outcomes and assess their own performance.

Assessment results of groups of students, schools, districts, and states will be available to the public. Teachers, administrators, boards of education, town and city officials, and state governments will be held accountable for results.

Statement of Beliefs

In writing the vision statement, the school is revealing its beliefs. Educators have always held certain beliefs or fundamental views toward all aspects of the schooling process. The planning team should stop at this juncture in the process and state those beliefs (see Figure 16.2). Although this may be done at the very beginning of the strategic planning process, there are many advantages to waiting until this point to reveal beliefs. Among these are the fact that team members are usually more forthcoming in revealing their beliefs after they have established a trusting relationship with the rest of the team. Also, after the steps of the planning process (external and internal scanning and organizational analysis), the team has developed a common vocabulary to use in describing beliefs. If the team has been attentive during these prior steps, it will choose terms familiar to the communities it is going to involve in writing the vision statement: the administration, faculty, students, and parents.

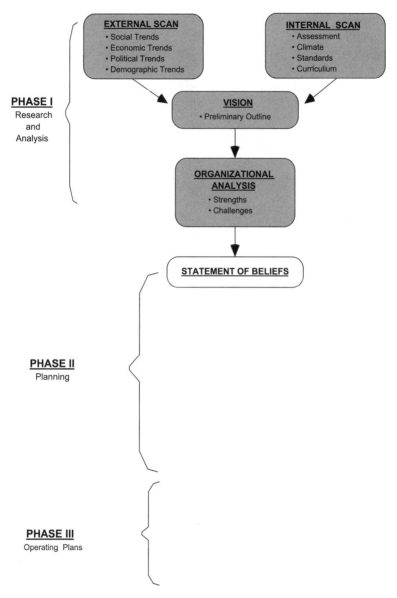

Figure 16.2. Strategic Planning Process

A belief, in this context, is an assumption upon which a person(s) acts. Thus, if a teacher believes that students can, in most circumstances, overcome their family problems and perform at acceptable levels, she has certain expectations of results. This belief colors the way she runs her classroom and the assessment (testing and grading) process she employs. One of the greatest problems in attempting to manage educational reform is that any given faculty may have as many different beliefs as there are teachers in that building. Educators are very hesitant to reveal their beliefs. Beliefs have not typically been part of the evaluation process. Teachers do not often hear their colleagues discussing them. They have not learned how one can discover one's beliefs during teacher training or through their supervisors. However, all teachers hold beliefs toward students, other teachers, curriculum, professional development, instruction, technology, governance, and information. This is the point where those beliefs should be revealed and shaped into commonly held beliefs.

Let us look at some possible beliefs that can come from this process. In the area of the student's role in the vision statement of the restructured school, the team might decide that two of its beliefs are that students should be seen as workers and that all students can succeed. Under the present school structure, these beliefs do not seem to be feasible. However, if the team really believes that they are a necessary component of a restructured school, they will write a vision statement that incorporates these notions. This vision might include references to evidence of the student as worker as being a decrease of teacher-centered activity and a commensurate increase in student-centered behaviors. The vision statement would also refer to a decrease in student dropouts and an increased performance of potential dropouts on standardized tests or some other local assessment tool.

Curriculum is another area that will reveal the different beliefs of the team members. Although most, if not all, will express the need for a stable curriculum, the real curriculum is not what is written but what is taught. Thus, internal scanning should pick up that certain aspects of the stated curricula are always taught and others are given scant acknowledgment. This is the point at which a team has to decide whether it wants to adopt a core curriculum, stating what is or is not to be in the core. Perhaps one of the reasons educators have in the past been hesitant to reveal their beliefs on curriculum reform is that they feared those beliefs would be interpreted as the rationale for elimination of one or more of their colleagues' positions. However, a vision statement has to reveal the beliefs of the planning team even when it will cause disruption. Schools can no longer afford to pretend to be all things to all people. They are now being asked to perform count-less tasks for society. If there are certain tasks the team believes the school cannot adequately achieve, this is the time to enumerate them and state what it can do well. Although there are certain tasks schools have thrust upon them, it behooves the team to identify the ones it feels are not in its purview to work with agencies better equipped to handle them. Educators cannot afford to be silent sufferers on this issue, especially as education budgets are being cut.

A final example of a belief is in the area of technology. If the team sees technology as having the potential of revolutionizing how students learn and how they are assessed, this should be revealed. Since many teachers do not believe this, at least not at present, the team needs to make it public that it holds this belief. Since this tenet is often a controversial one, it is a good example of why a team needs to reveal its beliefs. If a team believes this about technology, it must be able to present to the rest of the school, the parents, and the community why it holds this belief. Further, it should show how technology is now making a difference either in this school or at another school.

Revealing beliefs and building a consensus around them are difficult tasks for even the best of teams. However, the vision statement will be based on them. If the individual members have separate agendas, the vision will be fragmented and its impact minimal. Initially, the team might wish to reveal in writing what each member's beliefs are concerning the areas mentioned herein. Through discussion and editing a common set of core beliefs can be forged.

The Role of the School Librarian in Developing the School's Vision

As implied in *Empowering Learners: Guidelines for School Library Media Programs*, the school librarian should be viewed as the information expert within the school. If the school librarian is truly this expert, he has the obligation to ensure that the school's vision statement is written to reflect how the school is preparing students to live in an information age (*Empowering Learners*, 2009). Although the school librarian tends to be tuned into the rapid changes in information access, too many teachers and administrators are still receiving their information from the same sources they always have. If the history or algebra being taught is essentially what was presented 10 or 30 years ago, new information on the curriculum is not being used by the faculty. If the administration runs the building much as it was run in the previous generation, new information on governance (who is in control) and organization (schedules and teaming) is being ignored. More important, if students are not taught how to survive in the world of rapidly changing information, they will be ill prepared for the 21st century. Let us look at each of the sections of the school's vision statement and discuss what should be addressed to the satisfaction of the school librarian.

In the area of curriculum, the vision statement should mention the need for an information skills area. This need not be a separate curriculum area per se. It should, however, be a call for all areas of the curriculum to be responsive to the need for all people in an information age to become information problem solvers. Although this is more skill building than content (curriculum) development, it has its own skills continuum. Eisenberg and Berkowitz have shown how information problem solving can be taught across the curricula and from elementary school to the university (Eisenberg and Berkowitz, 1990). Although classroom teachers may think this area is important, it is the school librarian who is the best advocate of this approach. My experience has shown that board of education members and parents are the most enthusiastic supporters of this approach. They tend to realize, because of their own work situations, that information is power, and that the more empowered students become in this area, the better their chances of success. If the school's vision statement reflects needs of the present and future worlds, it will have to have a section on the need for an information skills curriculum. Even if it is not a separate curriculum area, it should be seen as an integral part of the other curricula.

The role of the student is one that moves away from the relatively passive role of receiver of predigested information to the active role of an information worker. Thus, the student is not only allowed to retrieve and manipulate information, she is encouraged to access information from various resources. After accessing it, she is expected to become an educated consumer of information. Specifically, she must evaluate the validity of the source. The student must compare and contrast this information to her prior knowledge to define the problem before her. She must gather the information from various sources and organize it in a presentable form. Last, the student should be able to evaluate how successful her research effort was and how she might improve on it the next time. The school librarian sees the need for the student to assume this role. The students who are successful with their research projects usually can define the problem, identify appropriate resources, extract needed information, organize and present the information, and are able to acknowledge how they might have improved their research if they could do it again. However, experience shows that most students fail in one or more of these areas. If we believe in success for all students, we have to develop a vision statement that explicitly describes what a knowledge worker does and how a student can become one.

The role of the teacher should address at least two aspects of information. Since all content areas are changing, the teacher whose knowledge base remains constant is one who is teaching inaccurate information. This is very obvious in the sciences, but it is also true for the Latin teacher. Second, the teacher whose source of information is the notes he took in college or the occasional conference he attended is not using the type of information accessing he needs to stay current. More and more teachers are networking, electronically and locally, to keep up. The school librarian should present the library as the logical focal point for such activity. Libraries should also be information centers for teachers.

The vision for the use of technology in the school should be one in which technology is presented as a tool to access, retrieve, manipulate, synthesize, and evaluate information. It is obvious that access to information will become progressively easier. The vision statement should acknowledge this trend and present how the school is going to approach this technology. Since the situation is rapidly becoming one of a plethora of information, even in the most inadequately funded schools, the school librarian should project where the school needs to be headed. A surfeit of information is as much a problem as inadequate resources. Both droughts and floods call for better management, though the technology may be different.

Finally, there should be a section on the role of the parents and the larger community. As mentioned before, parents or other community members who rely on current and accurate information in their careers will support the need for a section on preparing students to survive in an information age. Also, they will want to know what roles they will play in helping students succeed. If schools could once succeed without parental involvement and community support, they certainly can no longer. These same parents can, reciprocally, bring to the discussion of their child's educational plan some of the problem-solving techniques they employ in the workplace. Not only will they have a better appreciation of the educational process, they will be able to sell the value of the school's program to the greater public. The school librarian should use this as an opportunity to ensure that resource-based learning is presented as the most natural way to involve the greater community. The community can become the learning laboratory, preparing the students with the types of experiences they will need to be successful. By promoting this approach, an alliance between the school librarian and the ultimate decision makers in the community can be forged.

The Vision of the School Library

Concurrent with the formation of the school's vision is the creation of the library's vision. Although it will have more specifics on the importance of information in the education of students, it will complement the school's vision statement by drawing from the external and internal scan, recognizing the organizational analysis and reflecting certain aspects of the school's vision statement.

The vision of the library should be written with the success of the student as an information problem solver as its central theme. Since a vision statement should show where we are going by showing whence we came, a brief opening statement of what the library has been is a good way to set the stage for what it should become.

Although there are varying opinions on whether a discussion of the history of the library is necessary in a vision statement, it is my belief that it is an important element. Since libraries are moving away from being storehouses of materials and toward becoming learning laboratories, the vision statement should encapsulate this history. This is particularly important for the library since the other people involved in the planning process may not understand the magnitude of the change. If the school librarian truly believes that today's students find themselves in a world virtually flooded with information, the vision statement should present how the library is going to be profoundly changed by this information explosion. More important, it should show how its program will play an integral role in helping prepare students to become knowledge navigators in this sea of information. Next, there should be a presentation of the role of teachers and the school librarians. There should also be a projection of the role of technology. All of these elements should add up to a picture of what the library will look like in the future.

The vision statement of the library should show the unique contributions it will give to a restructured school. Since it should be considered the information center of the building, the whole school community should be using the library to train (students) or retool (teachers, administrators, and other adults) for the information age. If the student is to be understood as an information navigator or worker, there should be some discussion of the essential characteristics of this role. How will the student look in comparison to past attributes of a successful learner? A new set of skills has been emerging since the advent of *Information Power.* The student is seen as much more active and involved. Since he is learning to become an information consumer, we must look at how he develops strategies to acquire information, extracts the appropriate information, uses the best information, integrates that information into a presentable form, and evaluates the final product. This final stage of information consumption, evaluation, is an essential element of any vision statement. Not only must the individuals using the library evaluate their own work, but the library must evaluate its program. The vision statement should address what a successful program would look like and how it might be so judged.

Technology and the role it will play in changing the library cannot be overstated. Since virtually every major publisher of reference works is promoting or developing e-books, economics alone is going to dictate a shift toward electronics and away from print resources. So profound is the impact of just this one example of technological change that it would be difficult to imagine any vision statement without a significant section on the role of technology.

Since the school librarian plays a critical role in the development of the library program, there has to be some elaboration of his role in the process.

The vision is, indeed, his notion of what the library must become. Although this vision must fit with that of the school, it will have features unique to the perceptions of the school librarian. Just as only a local team can develop a vision for the school, so will the school librarian develop a unique vision of the library.

The local school librarian can take advantage of local, regional, state, and national organizations at this stage. Since other school librarians have developed vision statements for their programs, networking could be invaluable, since most of us are alone in our buildings. After such networks are accessed, different models of visions may be developed. This could have a very significant impact on the evolution of the role of the school librarian as a change agent in the restructuring of American schools.

The vision statement of the library should be brought to the school's planning team for review. For many members, it will be the first realization of the unique perspective of the school librarian. Hopefully, a dynamic dialogue on the role of the student as information problem solver will ensue. The vision may have to be revised one or more times so that it communicates to the team that which the school librarian intends. Team members may also be able to add their perspective on what will be required of students to succeed in an information age. The vision of the library should help the team focus clearly on that and other points raised by the school vision statement. Consider it a compliment if the team asks many questions and requests revisions. If they buy into this vision at this stage, they are much more likely to support the mission and action plans that come from it.

What follows is the vision statement I composed for a local library. Hopefully, it shows both its compatibility with the school's vision and the uniqueness of the library's program.

A VISION FOR THE LIBRARY

The vision of the future is of a library that would allow and promote access to information for all ability levels. This function would have as many systems as needed to allow for information to become "transparent," that is, available without a great investment of time and energy. Ultimately, the systems will merge into a unified access program capable of allowing the user to develop a lifelong dialogue with the human conversation.

In the past, emphasis has been placed on the library's role as a repository of books and other materials as well as that of supporting faculty and student use of nonprint media. This tended to combine two fairly dissimilar programs under the umbrella of "media center." The microcomputer has caused an irrevocable change for these functions. It appears that Web 2.0 tools such as wikis, browser-based multimedia, and social networking will only accelerate the pace of this change. Whereas research techniques (e.g., use of the card catalog) and the operation of equipment have been the main thrusts of most library programs, the future integration of information and the subsequent decrease of the barriers to attainment of information will call for a significant change or paradigm shift.

Sometime soon, artificial intelligence systems will answer most students' questions in a human-like manner or interaction. Exciting as this is, it will be tempered by the realization that these answers have to be seen as the product of a particular question. The question is more important than the answer. Ask the question slightly differently, and you will get a very different or even contradictory answer. Thus, the new skill will become the ability to ask the informed and intelligent question of the electronic oracle.

If we are in an information age, we have an obligation to teach our students to navigate through that information. A ship's navigator is not judged simply by his ability to read a compass or chart but by his facility in asking the appropriate questions of his instruments based on his understanding of the weather and the ship's systems and location. Our students must increasingly become aware of their environment (scanning); their own thought systems (metacognition); and where they are going (analysis, evaluation, synthesis, and creation of information). These are the habits of the knowledge navigator.

A metaphysical change is taking place. Whereas once we thought of the library program as centered in a place (library), we are moving into an era of electronic access no longer dependent upon being in a particular facility. Whatever is needed for the student to develop the ability to ask the right questions of the appropriate resources, regardless of location, is the focus of the new program. The challenge of the school librarian is to act as a change agent in this process. The school librarian remains the professional who is uniquely prepared to meet this challenge.

CHAPTER 17

The Mission Statement

If the school's mission is considered a distillation of the vision, writing a mission statement should be relatively straightforward. In addition, the process can be a great opportunity for collaboration on the part of the faculty. It helps establish a sense of purposefulness for all (Conley, 1992). The planning team should come up with two or three drafts of mission statements it can present to the entire faculty. Each should emphasize different elements of the vision. None should be longer than a paragraph. This would be another opportunity to convene two or three focus groups for the purpose of reviewing the statement to assess its ability to communicate the essential elements of the vision statement. The updated mission statements can be shared at a faculty meeting or specially designated planning day or workshop. This latter planning session will accomplish at least two things: it will foster a sense of ownership by the participants, and it is a means by which to see if the vision statement is truly understood.

The final phase of the mission statement is the phrases that come from it. There should be one for each of the major aspects. Each should be direct and unambiguous. They serve two purposes: they will be the basis for the action plans that follow, and they are a way of setting priorities for those plans.

If this process is done correctly, the short phrases of the mission statement become goals or objectives for the action plans. There will be a high degree of synergy between the vision and the objectives. The mission will be what the school is "about." If there are any phrases that are incompatible with the vision, it is the job of the planning team to correct this inconsistency.

The mission statement of Joel Barlow High School was developed after the vision statement was designed to reflect its essence.

Mission Statement for Joel Barlow High School

Joel Barlow High School is committed to developing a community of learners in which all students acquire the knowledge, skills, and confidence to meet the challenges of a changing society.

Thus, we will provide conditions that foster:

- an efficient organization, flexible and responsive to student needs

---

- an atmosphere of inquiry, encouraging exploration
- a dynamic curriculum, grounded in the values and traditions of our culture
- a high expectation of student success balanced by learner ability
- a diversity of learning strategies and opportunities that promote the intellectual, personal, and social development of each student

Since the final version of the mission statement is difficult for a group to compose, it would be wise for the planning team to appoint an editor. This person should be expert in the writing process, with a keen sense of how words fit together. Usually, language arts teachers are prime candidates. However, sometimes people who are used to writing grants or proposals are the best choices.

The completed mission statement should be sent to all communities involved with the running of the school, for editing purposes. If any part is ambiguous, it should be revised. It is paramount that the language be clear.

Revision of the Mission Statement

Once the mission statement has been accepted by all parties involved, it will not need to be revised as often as the vision statement. Mission statements are more global and tend to be tied to more stable truths about a school or a library then do vision statements. The latter tend to be much more connected to the external environment. If we think of McDonald's mission vis-à-vis its vision, we see that the mission has stayed intact for more than 50 years. However, the vision has had to adjust to the changing conditions of American society. Although the society still needs a clean, efficient, and reasonably priced restaurant, it now demands, among other things, an eatery that is environmentally and nutritionally conscious. McDonald's has responded to this shift in public preferences by promoting recycling and using less animal fat, as well as offering more healthy choices. As the character of America's eating habits changes, so, too, will the vision. However, the mission remains consistent. Perhaps there will come a need to change the mission, but this will happen only when a basic change in the vision has taken place. It would appear that this ability to change with society and still remain consistent with the mission is a prime reason for McDonald's phenomenal success.

Can the Mission Precede the Vision?

Obviously, one *could* write a mission statement before writing a vision statement. That mission statement might be inspiring and congruent with the philosophy of the school, but since it does not follow the vision, it has less of a chance of helping the school restructure itself.

Although the mission statement is not the most important step in the planning process, it should play the role of focusing on the essence of the vision statement. Mission statements are usually little more than platitudes, unless they are tied to the vision. It would have been a waste of time for McDonald's to have a mission without a vision. Although the McDonald brothers knew they wanted to sell fast food, their vision came from the experience of dealing with customers and attempting to make a profit. Their external scan told them that they were at the cusp of a change in the eating habits of Americans. It also told them that technology had advanced enough for them to design machinery that would allow them to turn a profit while selling inexpensive hamburgers. Their internal scan, or snapshot, told them that different aspects of their original operation (car hops, long menus, dishes) were inefficient. Their organizational analysis allowed them to jettison their inefficiencies and to begin to clarify their vision. Once this vision had taken shape and they both refined their systems and clarified their markets, their mission became clearer and more attainable. It would not have worked in reverse order because the mission is always secondary to the vision.

The mission of a school is less important and should follow the development of the vision. A mission amounts to little more than a pipe dream if it is not tied to the realities the vision statement has explored before it. However, if developed from the vision statement, it can become the common purpose for all involved (Joyce, Wolf, and Calhoun, 1993).

A Mission of the School Library

Just as the mission statement of the school reflects the core of its vision, so too does the mission statement of the library focus on the basics of its vision. Additionally, it should be compatible with the mission and vision of the school. However, since every area or department of a school should develop its own vision, this mission will have some unique aspects. Obviously, it will have to address the issue of information and access to it. I have found that the mission statement and phrases in *Empowering Learners: Guidelines for School Library Media Programs* can be helpful. Since the mission provides an excellent lens through which to view the information needs of the students, it would serve as a means by which to interpret the school's mission specific to the needs of an information society. As with the school's mission, it must contain the basic and more permanent elements of the library's vision.

What follows is an example of a mission statement of a library. It should be read in view of the vision and mission of the school and the vision of the library.

The mission of the library is to encourage students to develop the knowledge, skills, and confidence needed to navigate the sea of information.

Thus, we will provide conditions that foster:

- an efficient library, flexible and responsive to students' information needs
- an atmosphere of inquiry, encouraging information access
- a program consisting of the skills needed to efficiently and effectively access, extract, synthesize, and present information
- a high expectation of student success in using information
- a diversity of information technologies to allow for differing learning styles and abilities

---

If we look back at the vision statement of the library, we can see that this mission is derived directly from it. It contains the essence of the vision while emphasizing those aspects that tend not to change. Although the school's planning team might not necessarily take the initiative to emphasize information, this is a theme that flows through the school's vision statement and is an essential part of the library's vision.

The short phrases are directly connected to the library's vision, but they also parallel those of the school's mission statement. Although it is an elaboration of where the library wants to go, it also is designed to be harmonious with the school's direction. This synergy is the result of an integrated effort from the beginning. The school librarian, as a member of the planning team, understands the knowledge base (via the external scan) the team uses to make its decisions. In addition, the school librarian has apprised the team of the need to bring the school into the information age.

Since the planning team develops the school's vision and mission with all involved parties, the school librarian should offer the library's mission to it for comment and revision. The least this would accomplish is to show the team that this mission fits into the bigger picture of school reform. It will also be an opportunity for the school librarian to emphasize aspects of reform, such as information use, that other departments may not have highlighted.

The library's vision and mission should be a vehicle of change for the entire school. Schools tend to be oblivious to the demands of the information age. The challenge is for the school librarian to bring the planning team along to the point where they recognize the vision and mission of the library as being essential to the school's redesign. The next and final phase of strategic planning, the writing of the action plans, uses the bullets of the mission as goals or objectives. However, before the time and effort on the part of all involved in writing the action plans is spent, the planning team should adopt and make public certain givens or assumptions. Although there should not be many, they are the critical elements assumed for success of the strategic planning process.

School's Mission Statement	Library's Mission Statement
Joel Barlow High School is committed to developing a community of learners in which all students acquire the knowledge, skills, and confidence to meet the challenges of a changing society.	*The mission of the library is to encourage students to develop the knowledge, skills, and confidence needed to navigate the sea of information.*
Thus, we will provide conditions that foster: an efficient organization, flexible and responsive to student needs	Thus, we will provide conditions that foster: an efficient library, flexible and responsive to students' information needs
an atmosphere of inquiry, encouraging exploration	an atmosphere of inquiry, encouraging information access
a dynamic curriculum, grounded in the values and traditions of our culture	a program consisting of the skills needed to efficiently and effectively access, extract, synthesize, and present information
a high expectation of student success balanced by learner ability	a high expectation of student success in using information
a diversity of learning strategies and opportunities that promote the intellectual, personal, and social development of each student	a diversity of information technologies to allow for differing learning styles and abilities

---

Critical Assumptions

The planning team should, after the formulation of the vision and mission statements, look back at what has transpired and determine what would be essential for the success of the strategic planning process. Since in some schools it may take a year or more to reach this point in the planning process, outside and internal attention and criticism will probably be reaching a crescendo. Those outside the planning process will question whether anything worthwhile is happening. Along with reporting on the progress of strategic planning, the team should reveal its critical assumptions. The committee can use this spotlight to state what is needed for this process to continue and succeed.

What follows are the critical assumptions of the Joel Barlow High School planning team at this phase (see Figure 17.1). Note that there is a balance between more global issues and the specifics of action planning.

Critical Assumptions

- Change will be an ongoing, never-ending process.
- Teachers will continue to grow in their knowledge of content, their understanding of young people, their instructional expertise, and their courage to change.
- Teachers will be provided time for this growth and for the completion of the action plans.
- The community will commit itself to supporting the action plans with appropriate resources.
- The administration will continue to value this process as the main vehicle for restructuring the school.
- Individual teachers will feel free to decide on the degree of their involvement; membership on a committee or participation in a project will be voluntary.

Critical assumptions allow all to focus on the necessities of the planning process. Although some are exhortations to change and growth, others are requests for time and resources. If the board of education or superintendent cannot support requirements such as allowing planning days and paying for substitute teachers, this is the time to find that out. If the planning team has been in contact with the key players, these assumptions will not be a surprise. However, they will help clarify the necessities for continued success.

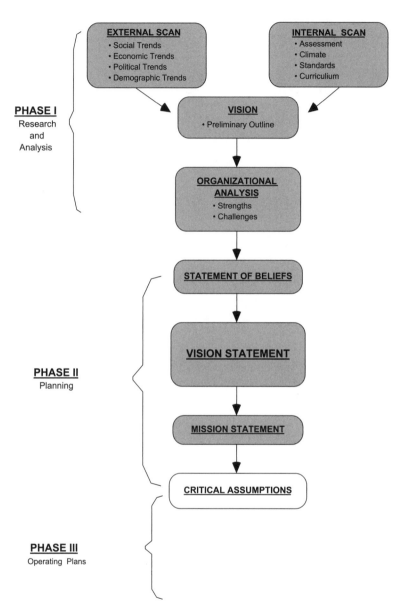

Figure 17.1. Strategic Planning Process

CHAPTER 18

Developing Action Plans

The final sequential step of the planning process is the writing of the action plans, which ensure that the strategies developed in the planning process are implemented (see Figure 18.1). They outline the tasks required to implement a program, the person responsible for each task, the due date for the completion of each task, and an analysis of the benefits and costs for the specific action plan.

The main intent in writing such plans is to address a particular issue raised in the vision and/or mission statements. Although the bullets of the mission statement should provide the major areas to be addressed in the action plans, it is possible to draw in other areas of focus from the vision statement. All plans will be subject to the scrutiny of priority, time considerations, resource availability, and feasibility. Therefore, it is best to draft as many plans as can be inspired by the vision and mission statements and limit their numbers later.

Each action plan should include the following sections:

- The issue (from the vision or mission statements) being addressed

- Tangible benefits

- Intangible benefits

- Critical assumptions on which the success of the action plan is based

- Evaluation criteria

- Start date

- Who is responsible for its completion

- Category and issue number

- Date of creation

- Statement of the problem it is written to address

- Action steps, with the person(s) responsible, start date, due date, and completion date

- Resource requirements/cost analysis

115

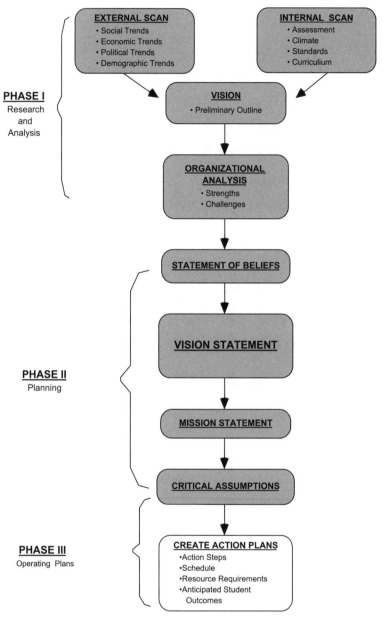

Figure 18.1. Strategic Planning Process

Before describing each of the elements of the action plans, it is important to realize how action plans function. An action plan's issue or area of focus is a theme that finds its roots in the organizational analysis. Remembering that the organizational analysis is the result of comparing the external scan with the internal scan, the issue an action plan attempts to address (or redress) is first identified at that stage. Let us trace an issue from the organizational analysis stage, through the vision and mission, to the action plan.

In the organizational analysis stage, the planning team determined that online learning was becoming a dominant component of the workplace and university setting. Since interest and involvement at the high school and university levels is welcomed and growing exponentially, it was chosen as an area to compare to the internal scan. A "snapshot" of the building and the district showed very little involvement with online learning. Because of this dissonance, it was deemed to be part of the organizational analysis. In listing it on the organizational analysis chart, there were some aspects mentioned on the strengths side. It was mentioned that some students were using online vendors for advanced placement courses. Others were using it for credit recovery. However, on the challenges side, various criticisms were rendered, the most important being that the school was not availing itself of online programs for any of the standard curriculum offerings. This is despite the consensus of the planning committee that success in the 21st century will require workers who can access and receive training through online offerings. Schools will have to expand their delivery methods to avail themselves of this important element of learning.

This issue is found in the vision statement in the following areas:

- Global: "Increasingly powerful technology will bring both the benefits and challenges of instant, far reaching communication."
- Local: "Parents will continue to demand vigorous and competitive academic preparation for their children, with considerable attention paid to individual needs. Technology will be accepted and expected."
- Institutional: "Specific changes can be expected in the use of technology, and in methods of instruction and assessment."
- Curriculum: "The organizing principle will be real life situations. The content will include a variety of cultures and viewpoints . . . transferable and marketable skills such as reasoning, problem solving, communication, and collaboration will be emphasized."
- Student Role: "The student will do actual research, gather information from various content areas."
- Teacher Role: "The teacher will be a co-learner, exploring issues and problems with students and sharing in research efforts."
- Technology: "As more and more information becomes available via technology, students will need to learn how to evaluate information quickly and determine what is useful . . . An important use for the computer in many disciplines is for the location and gathering of

information. There will be a movement from textbook orientation to a condition where, through a process of instantaneous information retrieval, students and teachers become discriminating consumers of a wealth of data . . . Satellite instruction, video conferencing, and computer networks will link Joel Barlow with other high schools . . . Administrative and guidance department applications of technology will increase. Career and college searches, data banks, and scheduling are just some of the anticipated uses."

- Instructional Strategies: "Specialized facilities such as the Writing Room, labs, and learning centers will be widely used."

- Assessment: "Students will be assessed on their level of knowledge and their skills in research, problem solving, collaboration, and communication, including listening."

Moving to the mission statement, we find in the text a reference to the need to develop learners who will "acquire the knowledge, the skills and the confidence to meet the challenges of a changing society." Within the mission's bullets, it is then mentioned that the school will provide conditions that foster:

"an efficient organization, flexible and responsive to student needs . . . a diversity of learning strategies and opportunities that promote the intellectual, personal, and social development of each student."

Thus, the issue of online learning has found its way from the external scan through the internal scan, organizational analysis, and vision and mission statements, and finally arrives at the action plan. As stated before, the action plan has many sections. The breakdown of these will be shown using online learning as an example.

Action Plan

Issue Being Addressed

As mentioned, the issue is restated, here, in its most specific form: online learning in the core academic areas

Tangible Benefits

Most action plans will have tangible or concrete benefits. In enumerating them, the committee is answering the "why" question, presenting the most provable rationale for proposing this action plan.

The tangible benefits of online learning are:

1. Increased access to course offerings.

2. Learning will not be tied to a rigid schedule of course offerings.

3. More optimal use of all networkable computers.

4. Accessibility through the Internet (school, home, or through wireless access).

Intangible Benefits

Although some benefits are not quantifiable, they are important and can help sell the action plan.

The intangible benefits of online learning are:

1. The faculty, students, and parents will see the learning as more accessible.

2. A greater sense of excitement about learning will be developed within the school, among parents, and within the whole community.

Critical Assumptions

Just as the success of strategic planning, in general, is based on certain critical assumptions, so too is the success of the action plan. It is the estimate of the planning team that without these pieces in place, the plan will not go forward. It is not suggested that there be more than two or three assumptions. However, they should be critical.

The critical assumptions for online learning are:

1. The community and board of education will provide the fiscal means to implement this action plan.

2. The technology exists to allow for the expanding of online learning offerings.

Evaluation Criteria

A strategic plan is assessed according to the value and efficacy of the individual action plans. If it did not have such a mechanism it would not be dynamic. Thus, the action plans should come with built-in evaluation criteria. Since the committee designing the action plan knows the most about its details, it should write the criteria. The method employed should be as concrete and obvious as possible.

The evaluation criteria for online learning are:

1. A special community composed of community members, administration, staff, and students will be convened.

2. A plan for the design, acquisition, and training will be produced by the previously mentioned committee.

3. Training opportunities will be provided for the staff.

4. Reports of curriculum changes and classroom practices indicating the use of online learning as an enhancement to student learning will be written.

5. Faculty, student, and parent surveys will be written to reveal the actual use of online learning.

Start Date

This is when the first action of the plan is to take place. Actions include not only implementation of the innovation but any of the research that goes into its preparation. If the intention is to start immediately, that should be unambiguously stated. For example, if the start date for expanding the use of online learning is this month, preliminary research should begin immediately.

Responsible Person(s)

A person or persons should be named. It is usually wise to avoid designating a group or committee since accountability is then too easily avoided. If a committee has to be mentioned, use the name of the chair or a prominent member.

Ideally, the assigned person takes part in the action plan writing or design process. Since these plans are going to need enthusiastic and creative shepherding from their coordinators, he should feel a sense of ownership as early as possible. The later the responsible person is brought into the process, the more difficult it will be to bring it to reality. Administering other people's plans is difficult for at least two reasons: the plan will probably not be fully understood, and it will be more difficult to identify with its success or failure.

If we are talking about online learning, the responsible person should be the director of school counseling. However, the school librarian could assume this role as well.

Category and Issue Number

For purposes of organization and classification, it is very useful to group all the initiatives coming out of the vision and mission into broader categories.

The major categories for the action plan might include curriculum, student role, teacher role, technology, instructional strategies, information use, communications, assessment, and governance/organization.

The school librarian can play an important role here by classifying the various plans into these broader categories. As a cataloger, his knowledge of information hierarchy and specificity will help the planning team identify duplication and inconsistency. A possible organization scheme one can use would be similar to Sears or Library of Congress headings and subheadings. The only caveat is to use terms that all the planning team members and the eventual participants will understand. Thus, our current example might become "Online learning" or subject heading, Internet in education. This should be interpreted to mean that this action plan is written to address the specific issue of online learning within the school under the umbrella of planning for technology improvement.

The breakdown of the areas might look something like this:

Curriculum

    1. Core Curriculum

    2. Interdisciplinary Units

    3. K–12 Skills Continuum

Student Role

    1. Student Writing

    2. Problem Solving

    3. Self-Assessment

Instructional Strategies

    1. Professional Development

    2. Models/Techniques/Strategies for Specific Content Areas

    3. Access/Distribution of Information on Instruction

Technology

    1. Using/Developing Technology for Students and Staff

    2. Computer Hardware/Software Acquisition and Training

Teacher Role

    1. Group Facilitator

    2. Teacher as Researcher

    3. Teacher as Content Expert

    4. Teacher as Curriculum Developer

Assessment

1. Student Portfolios
2. Process versus Product
3. Place of Traditional Tests and Measurements
4. Use of Assessment Results

Institutional (School Governance and Organization)

1. Community Involvement
2. Organization of Time (School Year and Day)
3. Area Specialists (Technology, Guidance, and Curriculum)

Communications

1. Use of the Media
2. Community's Perception of the School

Information

1. School as Information System
2. Use in Decision-Making Process
3. Information Skills

These last two areas, Communications and Information, are not sections of the vision statement, but they should be considered when developing action plans. Communications are important because the way in which strategic planning is presented to the greater community will determine its success. The most rational and elegant plan can be rejected by the board of education and the greater community if it is not presented in an understandable form.

School librarians know how important the area of information is. Although the vision statement may refer to information throughout its text, the school librarian should ensure that it becomes an area of focus for the action plans. Although there will be issues that involve the use of information in other areas, having it designated as a separate area is more of a guarantee of its eventual incorporation into the master plan for restructuring.

The category and issue number for online learning is Technology, #2–Online Learning.

Date of Creation

This is important vis-à-vis the start date. It not only shows how long the delay is between the conception and the start, but it supplies a reference point. In strategic planning, it is very important to know when plans are conceived. Since the conditions precipitating and affecting the plan will probably change, it may have to be revised or scrapped when the vision statement is updated. In this case, the date of creation would be the same as the start date.

Statement of Problem

This is the most important step in the action plan. If you can accurately state the problem to be addressed by the action plan, its solution will be much easier to bring about. When the team is writing an action plan, it would be wise to write the statement of the problem first. The effort involved in attempting to edit it down to an easily understandable sentence is a great opportunity for the group to sharpen its focus.

The statement of the problem for computer networks is: Since computer networks open students and staff to more information in a more efficient manner than do stand-alone computers, there is a compelling need to network the school's computers.

Action Steps

The final part of the action plan is the action steps. There should be as many as are necessary to bring the plan to completion. Each step should have: step number column, description of the steps column, "assigned to" column, a start date column, a date due column (if appropriate), a date completed column (if appropriate, see Figure 18.2).

Each of the boxes under the Action Steps heading should contain the following:

Step Number

The step number box is for a simple, sequential numbering reflecting the order of the initiation of the steps. Although there will be some steps that will be completed simultaneously or out of sequence, most will be done in the anticipated order.

There will be seven steps to create and develop a computer network for the school.

Action Steps

The action step box is for a brief (one to three sentences) description of the actual action or performance to take place.

Step one might read: "Preliminary research for the design, costs, and specifications of online learning system to be presented to a district technology committee for review."

Assigned To

This box names the person(s) responsible for its completion. I will later explain the participation of the responsible person who is important for this phase.

The director of learning resources and technology is responsible for the completion of most of the steps for developing an online learning program. The computer coordinator will also be assigned some of the steps.

Start Date

A box will contain the start date of each of the steps. Obviously, the first box will have the same date as the start date of the action plan.

Due Date

The due date will test the committee's ability to estimate a completion date. Although some steps will be ongoing, most will have end points. The first estimates will probably be inaccurate. However, the experience of seeing the plans develop over a few years will tend to teach the art of estimating time. Thus, each step will have its estimated date of completion.

Date Completed

The actual date of completion is entered in this box. Over the course of time, this box will help the planning team understand which type of tasks tend to be completed within a predicted time and which tend to need more time. Since estimating the time required is not always easy, these boxes provide the planning team with important data. When entered into a spreadsheet program, these data help to track the progress of action plans. This will cause the team to review and monitor plans that are not on pace. Some action plans will have to be altered or scrapped because of changes in the external environment. An example might be a new state mandate that runs counter to the direction of the action plan. There could also be a change in the internal world (the school) that causes the elimination of a plan. If, for example, the person responsible for the completion of the plan had his position eliminated, the plan would probably not be completed. Such a plan would probably not have a completion date and would have to be reviewed as soon as possible.

Resource Requirements/Cost Analysis

The two most precious resources of most schools are money and time. Most plans will have to estimate both. Because of the growing scarcity of these resources, estimates should be as realistic as possible.

Action Plan

Start Date _____   Strategy Number _____

Responsible (name) _____

Date _____

Issue: _____
_____

Statement of Problem: _____
_____
_____
_____

Step No.	Action Step	Assigned to:	Start Date (if appropriate)	Date Due (if appropriate)	Date Completed (if appropriate)

Figure 18.2. Strategic Planning Process

The money could come from a reallocation of existing funds or a request for new funding. Since budgets are usually proposed 6 to 18 months before the money can be spent, the start date will be different for newly appropriated monies in contrast to reallocated dollars.

The planning committee may need help from administrators on the committee who are familiar with the planning process. Obviously, there will be a need to total the cost of all the action plans and their time requirements before the priority-setting process occurs.

The cost analysis for beginning and maintaining a virtual (online) learning program would be:

1. $20,000 in the first year — $14,000 for .2 FTE (full-time equivalent teacher); $5,000 for teacher training; and $1,000 for miscellaneous fees

2. $15,000 in the second year — $14,500 for .2 FTE teacher and $500 for miscellaneous fees

3. $15,500 in the third year — $15,000 for .2 FTE teacher and $500 for miscellaneous fees

4. $30,500 in the fourth year — $30,000 for .4 FTE teacher and $500 for miscellaneous fees

5. $31,500 in the fifth year — $31,000 for .4 FTE teacher and $500 for miscellaneous fees

Who Writes Action Plans?

Research indicates when there is a high level of participation on the part of multiple participant groups, educational strategic planning is viewed as effective by these groups (Conley, 1992). If the previous steps have been followed with an eye toward participation of all parties, or what some might call the stake holders, this phase will be the most inclusive of all. When looking at a school, the action plan development stage should be something everyone who wishes to can be a part of. The board of education, the administration, teachers and other staff members, students, parents, and interested community members should have the opportunity to become involved in the design of action plans (Saphier, Bigda-Peyton, and Pierson, 1989).

This high level of participation is important for many reasons. Not only does it develop a sense of ownership in the strategic planning process, but it functions as an important review of the meaning and understanding of the vision and mission. In the next chapter, it will be shown how each action plan will be held up against public scrutiny, which includes agreement with the vision and mission statements. The higher the level of participation in the writing of the plan, the greater the likelihood of identification with the success of not only the individual plan but the entire strategic planning process. Since it will probably be disruptive to the school day to have so many people involved in planning, having a few planning days over the course of the school year may work well. Although these could be consecutive days, there is greater efficiency in having them spaced throughout the year. This will test the will and resources of most school districts, but the benefits accrued will be many.

For purposes of organization and consistency with the previous steps, it is suggested that the categories previously mentioned (curriculum, student role, instructional strategies, technology, assessment, institutional issues, communications, and information) be used. Since some people will want to serve on more than one action plan writing committee, either a lottery system could be used or the day could be split up with half of the areas in the first session and half in the second. Each committee should have an elected chair and a facilitator. It would be helpful to make a representative of the strategic planning team the facilitator. This will increase the chances of an accurate interpretation of the planning committee's intent and increase everyone's sense of ownership in the strategic planning process.

The School Librarian and Action Plans

If the school librarian has gone through the previous steps of strategic planning for the library, this will be a point of convergence for what had been parallel planning tracks. Since the apex of strategic planning is the action plans, the school librarian should put a great deal of effort into seeing that some of the school's action plans involve him. If he writes and edits the action plan, this would be even better. The ultimate object is for him to be involved in at least two or three action plans.

Ideally, the action plans the school librarian is involved with will come from the vision and mission statements of the library. Since they should be related to the mission and vision of the school, they are the result of the ongoing synergy that has existed in the planning process between the whole school and the library. The library and any of the other departments are not pressure groups or special interests. Strategic planning's intent is to break down the traditional turf wars that one experiences in most schools and to focus on the bigger picture, the vision. Since the school librarian usually represents the smallest department in the school, his talents as a team player and collaborator should be employed. The action plans the school librarian is involved in must be viewed as vital to the future of the school.

Although the library will have its own action plans, most of the energy of the school librarian should be employed in collaborating with others to write action plans for the entire school. If the school librarian collaborates in the writing of two or three action plans for the school, there should be at least as many others, specifically for the library. The school-wide action plans should have a direct connection to the vision or mission statements. The ones for the library should be connected to the vision or mission of this function. An example of an action plan, specifically for the library, might be: An analysis of the library's systems should be conducted to determine their flexibility and responsiveness to student information needs. As with all action plans, there would be a progression through the various parts.

Issue Being Addressed

Although we are the main authors and audience of this plan, we should still present the issue as plainly and directly as possible. We may want to present the action plan to an administrator or to a volunteer who is helping us.

Tangible Benefits

The anticipated concrete benefits of this action plan will be:

1. Systems more responsive to student habits will be devised and put into place.

2. A baseline for future data analysis will be established.

3. The results will be used in the internal scan of the strategic plan of both the library and the school.

Intangible Benefits

As a consequence of this action plan, it is expected that the following, less quantitative results will occur:

1. Students will be more inclined to use the library.

2. The school librarian will have a better awareness of the value and time requirements of systems analysis.

Critical Assumptions

To be successful, it is assumed that:

1. Someone knows or has time to learn enough about systems analysis to be able to collect and evaluate the appropriate data.

2. Clerical support is available for data collection.

3. Computer analysis can greatly aid the process.

Evaluation Criteria

In order to determine the success of the action plan, the following criteria will be used:

1. A plan for doing a systems analysis will be devised.

2. The school librarian will make a report on the systems of the library and enact appropriate changes.

Start Date

To work this task into our busy schedules, it is important to establish when we are beginning the innovation.

Responsible Person(s)

Even though the school librarian(s) will be responsible for the completion of most of the steps of the action plan, it is important to anticipate if it will affect other members of the library's staff.

Category Code or Number

The school librarian can determine whether or not to use an internal coding system. It is recommended that if one is adopted it function much like the school's coding system.

Date of Creation

Although we might have conceived this plan alone or among school librarians, it is a good practice to note when we did. Busy schedules can cause us to lose track of time. We become better planners when we see how long plans actually take from conception to completion.

Statement of Problem

The statement of the problem this action plan is attempting to address should discuss its importance vis-à-vis the other initiatives in the library:

With the proliferation of information systems available, it becomes increasingly difficult to assess which ones are closest to the information retrieval habits and abilities of the students. Since this is a key component in the success of student research, an analysis of the existing systems in the library and other possible systems is required.

Action Steps

Each action step is described in an action step box.

Step one (of five) would read, "A review of the literature of systems analysis for library systems will be conducted to determine the best approach to take."

Assigned To

Although one person will be assigned to coordinate this action plan, others will be involved.

Start Date

Each step's start date will coincide with the previous and subsequent step, as much as possible.

Due Date

Although estimating due dates can be difficult, this is a good experience in acquiring the ability to gauge how long such plans take to complete.

Resource Requirements/Cost Analysis

The equipment, supplies, personnel costs, training, and staff development should be estimated for the duration of the action plan.

CHAPTER 19

Setting Priorities

The most contentious and difficult step in the strategic planning process is deciding which plans will receive the most attention. A process should be established that is fair to all concerned. This decision-making scheme will involve the vision and mission, feasibility, student outcomes, budget implications, and short-term versus long-term implementations. Each action plan will be looked at through these various "filters" before deciding which will receive the highest priority and which will have to wait for a better time.

This stage should be a very public one as well. A perception on the part of the various participants that an elite group is pulling the strings of priority setting can doom the action plans. Indeed, after discussing the various criteria, there will be a presentation on how to get the highest level of faculty and community participation in the decision-making process.

Mission and Vision Statement

To be consistent will the rest of the strategic planning process, the first screening step is to look at the action plan in comparison to the vision and mission statements. Although such a comparison should have been taking place throughout the planning process, it is possible that an action plan will be proposed that does not seem to receive support from the vision or mission. Unless that plan can be revised through negotiations between the planning team and the action planning committee, it should receive the lowest priority. Plans that are easy to write and inexpensive to enact but do not have any real connection to the vision or mission statements are not going to move the school where it wants to go. Since it will be necessary to review many action plans, it would be useful to rate each of these on a high-priority to low-priority scale. A 1–6 scale for this and the other categories will be helpful in determining the final priority order.

Feasibility

After deciding how closely the action plan conforms to the vision or mission, it will then have to be scrutinized according to its feasibility. Rarely will a school be able to avoid the realities of budgets, time requirements, understanding on the part of those who must enact the action, along with other real world considerations. Even if an action plan had a high mark for its synergy with the vision or mission, if it receives a low feasibility rating, it will probably be crippled from the start.

The main elements for judging an action plan's feasibility are:

Budget. How much money does it require to initiate or maintain as compared to existing or potential resources?

Time. Can this task realistically fit within someone's schedule or can a new position be created?

Expertise. How much specialization is required and does such expertise exist within the present staff?

Measurable Student Outcomes

The final screening process involves what strategic planning for education is intended to address: improvement of student performance. Because of the situation in which American education finds itself, we have to remind ourselves that the public who pays the taxes is looking for results. Although educators know that much of what happens in the education process is not readily quantitative, the spotlight of the media and most politicians will be on tangible results. Therefore, this, the third of the criteria for acceptance of action plans, has to have equal importance with the first two.

Having the screen of measurable student outcomes also acts as a safety net for the planning process. Student learning will increase only when that is a central goal of the action plan (Joyce, Wolf, and Calhoun, 1993). The committee designing the plan will know that concrete results will be one of the three major areas of the assessment of the plan. A plan may seem to be very close to the vision or mission and have a high feasibility rating, but it might have outcomes that are difficult to demonstrate. Having this criterion will tend to keep the critics of school reform in check. Strategic planning could look too much like another bureaucratic exercise if most of the action plans do not point to changes that can be seen and measured within a year or two after enactment.

Who Judges?

The most crucial decision a planning team has to make at this phase is who will have the power to approve the various action plans? Although the planning team can opt to reserve this process for itself, it is important not to seem to be elitist. Not only is elitism bad politics, it will probably not give the school the best set of action plans that divergent viewpoints tend to give.

In order for an inclusive process to take place and for the planning team to retain the necessary control, focus groups can be used once more. There should be no more than four groups, each with no more than five members, one of whom should be a member of the planning team. Each focus group should have the criteria for priority setting of action plans explained to it by the entire planning team. This will tend to save time, and everyone will have a similar understanding of the selection process.

Using a numerical rating system of high to low (6 to 1) approval for each of the three criteria, the action plans should be numbered from highest acceptance (18) to lowest (3). Once each focus group has ordered the plans, there should be a meeting of all the focus groups and the planning committee. The spokespeople or chairs of the focus groups should present their judgments with explanation. There will, no doubt, be a lively discussion about the different ranks and understanding of the value of the plans. Since this can be a very sensitive juncture for the many people who have invested time and energy in writing the action plans, the planning committee has to take much of this discussion under advisement. If there is any doubt about the meaning of the text of any of the action plans, the planning team or its representative should not hesitate to ask the original authors.

Since this will be the first time that many staff or community members will have an opportunity to propose a plan for the school, great care has to be taken to ensure that they understand why their particular plan is rejected or modified. Besides striving for the best action plans, it is equally important to have people who are committed to the strategic planning process. Since the planning team should have a rotating membership, these people will be asked to serve on it at some future time. They will not want to serve if they do not believe the planning process is a fair and equitable one.

The final step in the action plan phase is for the planning team to take all the previous proceedings into account and to make its final decision as to which plans to go with and which to either alter, postpone, or scrap. This is the moment of truth in the planning process. Hopefully, most plans' acceptability will seem to be obvious after this exhaustive review process. However, there will probably be an action plan or two that receive either too high or too low a rating. The committee must exert itself and propose the plans in the order it sees fit.

Final Deliberation

The planning committee must come up with a priority listing. Short of an unanticipated windfall, it will know a line below which plans will not make the cut for funding and support. Before dooming a plan to ignominy, there are at least two ways to save it. The first is to combine it, or at least elements of it, with similar but higher ranked plans. The second is to phase it in over a longer time than originally proposed.

Through creative editing, the planning team can combine parts of action plans that do not receive high enough ratings with a highly rated plan. Although this should be done only when such an addition is seen as strengthening the accepted action plan, it serves a multitude of purposes. It tends to show the whole school that there are certain shared themes or unities. It allows a particularly exceptional step of an otherwise lowly rated plan to be adopted. Finally, and most important, it tells the committee that wrote the action plan that its thoughts and work are valued.

What follows is an example of the evaluation process using the previously described online learning plan. The committee that wrote the action plan for an online curriculum made an excellent case for giving this plan the highest rating, 6, because of its high agreement with the vision and mission of the school. In defending it to the focus groups and later to the planning team, it cited the following specific sections of the vision and mission statements:

Vision statement:

"Increasingly powerful technology will bring both the benefits and challenges of instant, far reaching communication."

"Parents will continue to demand vigorous and competitive academic preparation for their children, with considerable attention paid to individual needs. Technology will be accepted and expected."

"Transferable and marketable skills such as reasoning, problem solving, communication, and collaboration will be emphasized."

"The student will do actual research and gather information from various content areas."

"The teacher will be a co-learner, exploring issues and problems with students and sharing in research efforts."

"As more and more information becomes available via technology, students will need to learn how to evaluate it quickly and determine what is useful."

"There will be a movement from textbook orientation to a condition where, through a process of instantaneous information retrieval, students and teachers become discriminating consumers of a wealth of data."

"Students will be assessed on their level of knowledge and their skills in research, problem solving, collaboration, and communication, including listening."

Mission statements:

"An efficient organization, flexible and responsive to student needs."

"A diversity of learning strategies and opportunities that promotes the intellectual, personal, and social development of each student."

Thus for agreement with the vision and mission, computer networking received a rating of 6 from the focus groups.

The initiation and maintenance of an online learning program proved to be problematic. Looking at the three major areas of feasibility rating (budget, time, and expertise), the online learning program did not appear highly feasible under existing economic circumstances. It required more time than it appeared people had to give. Finally, although the existing director of independent and online learning was doing a creditable job, it appeared that he would require intensive training to be able to administer an online or virtual learning program.

The focus groups gave the action plan a 3 for feasibility. They felt this action plan deserved a relatively high rating in the area of measureable student outcomes. They noted that there is not too much known about the effect of online learning on student outcomes, especially in the core areas. Looking at online learning programs in other school districts and the indications that these programs tend to increase measureable student outcomes, the focus groups decided to give the action plan a rating of 5.

With a cumulative score of 14 out of a possible 18, this plan did not have a high enough rating to receive first-priority status. The planning team was interested in making it a high-priority plan since it was rated so highly in the vision/mission area and in measureable student outcomes. However, in order to do this, it had to address the area of feasibility.

To apprise them of the situation, the planning team called in the authors of the action plan: the school librarian, the computer coordinator, and the director of guidance. The planning team asked the committee to come up with an answer to the issues of time and expertise and to report back in two weeks. It decided to address the issue of budget directly with the superintendent and board of education.

After some deliberation, it was decided by the board of education and the administration to form a special committee of parents, teachers, and administrators to get the support within the community to pay for this program. This committee was given the action plan to review and revise if necessary. It was also made clear from the start that the money needed to initiate and maintain an online learning program could not be added to an existing budget and had to be appropriated some other way. The board and administration also made it clear to this special committee that, within certain limitations, a multiphase approach was the most acceptable.

The action plan writing committee reported back to the planning team that it felt the issues of time and expertise were not as insurmountable as had originally been thought. In doing research and calling schools with online learning programs, it was discovered that the regional educational cooperative could assume some of the budget for the first year of the teacher and his training.

This example illustrates the role of the planning team vis-à-vis action plans. Although there was a very high degree of participation on the part of the faculty in the writing and rating of this plan, the planning team played the pivotal role of bringing a plan that was very close to the vision and mission of the school into reality. It did not ignore the difficulties in the area of feasibility. Instead, it looked for creative ways of overcoming these obstacles.

CHAPTER 20

Action Plans and Budgetary Considerations

Ideally, the action plans will become a major part of the budgeting process. Since strategic planning reveals the priorities of the school and where it intends to go, the rest of the budget can be built around it. However, most schools find themselves in situations that do allow for such a seamless transition from traditional budget to a strategically developed one.

Since the budgeting process is usually set by forces outside the school (state, county, or district regulation), action plans usually fit best into areas of the budget that allow for program improvement. Although strategic planning will ultimately call for a thorough revision of the budgeting process, there is usually a period of adjustment.

This is the point where the greatest support and involvement on the part of the administration are needed. If the superintendent or her delegate has been involved from the beginning in the strategic planning process, she should be able to advise the planning team on the best approach to take in dealing with the existing budgeting process. She and the board of education representative(s) should have been informing the board of the intents and outcomes of the planning process. It is, however, an excellent idea for the entire planning team to make a presentation to the board at a scheduled meeting. Since the support of the board is usually essential for the success of the plan during the budgeting process, its members should understand the importance of the strategic plan as a means to make the school into the type of organization that can best prepare its students to be successful citizens in the 21st century.

The school librarian should help design this presentation to the board. Since the vision is the most important aspect of the plan, use of engaging and clear visuals or a video can help the board realize where the school is going. The school librarian is usually the person on the team who has the most experience with audiovisual presentations. Even if the eventual presentation is professionally produced, the school librarian can use all of his various professional contacts to ensure that the most effective presentation is what

137

the board sees. Although the planning team could wait to present to the board when the action plans are complete, it is advised that the presentation take place soon after developing the vision and mission statements for at least three reasons: (1) The planning team is closest to the vision and is most enthusiastic soon after developing it; (2) The team is going to have to ask the board for support in the action plan development stage; (3) The budget the board will next see will have a priority set by the strategic planning process. It needs to become familiar with the nomenclature of strategic planning, understanding what such terms as *vision statements* and *organizational analysis* mean.

Since most budgets are divided into departments or object codes, the library account will be selected to show what happens to an area when it is altered by the strategic planning process. All other departments or areas of the school should adopt a similar format. What follows is an example of a library's budget after going through the strategic planning process.

The Budget and the Library

The first part of the library's budget is its vision and mission statements. This establishes what the librarian hopes this budget will begin to bring to reality. It also sets a tone of strategic, long-range planning. Although the nuts and bolts of maintaining the library's many functions (buying books, repairing equipment, processing materials) will be part of the budget, the vision and mission set a higher tone for it defense. All new initiatives should be directly related to the vision.

Next comes the organizational analysis. Since this addresses the present and the future, it is an excellent transition from the vision and mission to the "dollars-and-cents" section. The organizational analysis communicates to the board what is strong within the present program and what is a real or potential problem. By listing the strengths the board is able to understand that past funding has brought benefits the school librarian intends to keep, whenever possible. The challenges section emphasizes where the school librarian intends to go. Every one of the challenges should be connected to the vision and/or mission statements of the library, which are in turn connected to the vision and mission statements of the school. There should not be any surprises or incongruities. This, in effect, establishes the priorities of the library program. If cutbacks have to take place, new initiatives will have at least as high a priority as existing programs. The vision has to be seen not as "nice if you can afford it," but a necessary step in taking the school where it must go. The board should understand that when it cuts sections or percentages of this budget, it is keeping the school from where it needs to be. Conversely, by identifying the priorities of the library, the school librarian must be prepared to cut in areas of lower priority. This may involve positions and programs that the school has taken for granted. The strength of the strategic planning process is that it tends to view budgets as unified wholes rather than as a compilation of many competing departments or fiefdoms. Areas that have very little to do with the vision or mission of the school should see their support dwindle over the years of budgeting.

Following is an example of an organizational analysis written especially for a budget presentation:

Analysis of Present Status of Department Activities in Comparison to the Vision Statement:

Library	
CHALLENGES	**STRENGTHS**
Introductory Statement With the accelerating pace of technological change, it becomes more difficult to choose the most appropriate systems.	The present systems allow for more access to information for all ability levels than any in the past.
Student Role The student must increasingly become an independent researcher. At present, students do not take full advantage of the library. There is a need to continue to develop a grade 9–12 research program.	The students who take advantage of the library are able to access information electronically and manually.
Teacher Role At present, about two-thirds of the faculty has been trained in the use of computers to access information.	Between 10 and 20 teachers are being trained each year in the professional development workshops "Electronic Access to Information."
Technology Although the technology allows for more access to information than ever before, we have five different research databases. Even with their many similarities, there is a need for integration.	We have a student body that welcomes technological innovations. Federated search engines are available to do a unified search of many of our subscription databases.

Instructional Strategies The library and the Writing Center have formed a research committee to create a systematic approach to the teaching of research skills.	Each student gets individual attention when learning the new systems of electronic access. We require every ninth-grader to take a week-long research program.
Assessment There is a need to assess whether students can perform independent research. Specifically, a scoring rubric has to be designed to measure the research process.	Pre- and post-tests are used to assess student progress in learning information skills.
Staffing The professional staffing level is inadequate. State guidelines recommend having 3.5 (full-time equivalent) professionals.	The support staff of the library is highly competent and dedicated.

Since the per-pupil expenditures budget account is normally the most secure, or the last to be cut, those sections with the highest priority in the vision, mission, and organizational analysis of the library should find themselves here. If the budget is composed mostly of line items that reflect maintenance of existing programs and functions, it is obvious that it does not reflect strategic planning. Even if an action plan can be phased in over two or more budgets, it would still be strategic.

Although long-term contractual obligations cannot be changed in the budgeting process, there is often a section of the budget that deals will new expenses, such as capital improvements, curriculum improvement, or professional development. This part should be dedicated exclusively to action plans. Since the school librarian rank ordered these action plans, they should be defended with that order of importance in mind.

In summary, even though there is an attempt to preserve as much of the existing program of the library as possible, the new budget will reflect as much of the strategic plan as possible. Especially in difficult financial times, the *library* cannot be seen to be initiating programs that are not integral to the greater strategic plan. Even the maintenance of certain existing programs and personnel might have to be sacrificed for the greater good. This will tend to solidify the position of the school librarian as a strategic planner and team player.

CHAPTER 21

Keeping Strategic Planning Dynamic

To sustain strategic planning's dynamic nature in the school setting, three areas should be promoted: understanding the relationship among the parts of the planning process, learning about the change process, and professional development. Without each of these becoming a part of the life of the school, the plan will become static and soon join other educational reforms in the graveyard of good intentions.

Relationship Among the Parts of the Planning Process

The first time through the planning process, it is necessary to go through the various steps sequentially. However, this linear approach is mostly for purposes of learning and team building. Once the planning team has all the steps completed, it is no longer a sequential process. Although external scanning will be required continually, it is not a matter of "returning to go," as in the game of Monopoly. Rather, it and the other steps become subsystems to the process of strategic planning. Just as the various subsystems of the body (circulatory, respiratory, etc.) function simultaneously, so too should the elements of the strategic plan. Thus, the team should have ways of monitoring the external environment and the internal world of the school and be thinking how these affect the organizational analysis. The vision will change as the organizational analysis is altered. Although the mission may not change very much, its dynamism comes from its serving as a touchstone against which the action plans are held when they have to be reviewed because of changes in the vision. As action plans will have to be changed when the other parts are altered, they can also cause the other elements to be rewritten. Thus, the mistakes made in the design and implementation of action plans become the necessary data the planning team needs to adjust and revise. Failure is inevitable. Learning from these problems is the challenge

141

to keep the plan dynamic. Problem solving is the main task of the planning team after the initial planning process (Joyce, Wolf, and Calhoun, 1993). All parts are intimately connected. A change in one either causes a change in the others or is caused by their alterations.

The planning team retains primary responsibility for updating the elements of the plan. It can appoint one of its members or a member of the school community to oversee a step. Indeed, the school librarian would be an ideal monitor of the external environments. However, the planning team must constantly review the data as they come in. Certain warning signs might appear on the horizon of the external world. The person monitoring and the entire planning team will have to learn which signals to heed and which simply to continue observing.

Since the vision statement is so vital to the success of the plan, great care should be taken in overseeing its revision. Although a revision is easier than the first vision statement, the planning team should appoint a subcommittee to revise it every two to three years. With the external environment changing at a very rapid rate, the vision will have frequent substantive changes.

The Change Process

Although it would be helpful for anyone trying to deal with today's hectic world to understand the change process, it is essential for everyone involved in strategic planning to do so. Research on schools that are attempting to restructure themselves points to the need to help the participants understand what is happening to them as they change and to others whom they are asking to change (Joyce, Wolf, and Calhoun, 1993). If you are to understand and prepare for each of the predictable stages of the change process, you must understand what those steps are.

Often planners forget that when they first attempted an innovation they had high levels of concern throughout the learning and implementation process until the innovation became internalized. Some of the most important findings concerning educators' response to the stages of the change process come from the works of Hall and Hord (Joyce, Wolf, and Calhoun, 1993). Using a seven-stage model of change based on the concerns of teachers at each step, they have come up with a comprehensive approach for dealing with practically anyone at any stage of the innovation (Hall and Hord, 1984, 52–79). If we do not recognize at what stage of the change process an individual or group of individuals is, we will not know the proper interventions to employ. If an individual is telling us that he is at the orientation or initial learning phase and we respond with an intervention more appropriate to a more advanced stage, we will alienate him from the strategic planning process. People do not usually adopt an initiative unless they see its inherent value. They will not understand and value such an initiative unless they can try it out. This is especially true for a relatively unfamiliar innovation such as strategic planning. Public bureaucracies, such as public education, have traditionally been concerned more with maintenance than development. However, we cannot have progress without change (Perelman, 1988).

The success or failure of this planning process hinges on whether a critical mass of the faculty of a school adopts at least some key elements of the plan. Schools change only after enough individuals in them adopt those changes. Both the planning team and all participants in the strategic planning process should be given training in the change process (Joyce, Wolf, and Calhoun, 1993). Since the stages of change are essentially the same whether or not the persons initiate the innovation or have it thrust upon them, understanding this process helps individuals retain some level of control over its implementation. The most elegant plans can be rejected by faculties who do not receive the type of information and support required at their stage in the change process (Joyce, Wolf, and Calhoun, 1993). Although there may be some faculty members who will fight virtually all changes, most resistance is the communication of the natural anxiety felt when attempting something new. Since teachers have to be concerned with not only how they will manage an innovation but how their colleagues and students will view them during this phase, it is not surprising that they can get so apprehensive. Changes in the past have failed not only because they appeared to be "top-down" and not connected to the reality of the classroom; they also failed because the necessary support to bring teachers through the stages of change was rarely present (Fullan, 2000).

Professional Development

The third *sine qua non* in keeping the strategic planning process dynamic is professional development. Strategic planning is most effective when it is used to coordinate the various initiatives in the building. These innovations usually come as a result of the professional growth of a group of teachers. Professional growth empowers educators and gives them a sense of involvement in the destiny of the school (Dunsworth and Billings, 2009, 122–125). If an individual is becoming proficient in cooperative learning, he will value the work of strategic planners because of the collaborative nature of the endeavor. Those who are growing in the area of process writing will respect the vision statement and action plans as exercises in bringing meaning to concepts and notions via the written word. Those who feel technology will be the engine that drives change in education will applaud the prominence strategic planning gives it. Even the educator who is becoming more proficient in her discipline will be able to see that most subject areas are writing or implementing national standards that are strategic in that they are responding to national educational goals and initiatives. The process of strategic planning eventually has to become the property of the whole community. Professional development is the fertile ground from which strategic planning sprouts. Since emphasis in professional development is moving away from a search for formulas of skills and toward understanding how to develop problem solvers, we will become the problem solvers any organization needs to succeed (Joyce, Wolf, and Calhoun, 1993).

The strategic planning team needs to work in an environment where all members of the school community are involved in lifelong learning. From time to time, it also needs some specific training in the planning process. As mentioned earlier, the team should become expert in understanding the change process. In addition, someone on the team should become the process champion (Conley, 1992). In other words, someone should research and become reasonably proficient in the strategic planning process. There are presenters who offer workshops on strategic planning that these process champions can attend. In addition, organizations such as the Association for Supervision and Curriculum Development sponsor networks for individuals interested in sharing experiences in strategic planning.

The final aspect of professional development is the use of external consultants. The reason that this is considered part of professional development is that the consultant is not to be viewed as someone who writes the plan for the school. Rather, he is paid to facilitate the process of strategic planning. In addition, he should teach the critical elements of the process and help the team evaluate them. Since every school will have a plan unique to its circumstances, he can function to remind the team what strategic planning hopes to accomplish. The best of these consultants do not come with preconceived ideas about what specific issues and answers will emerge from the process. Rather, they convey confidence that the process will result in good answers and help those answers to appear (Conley, 1992). At least in urban situations, it was found that a minimum of 30 days of such external assistance was required to ensure success (Fullan, 2000).

CHAPTER 22

Caveats and Serendipity

Although this presentation of the strategic planning process seems fairly simple and straightforward, schools are anything but simple systems to reform. Because of their complexity and the seeming inability of reforms to stick, there are five warnings and some benefits of the planning process that should be noted. This process requires a substantial amount of time, funding, and influential administrators. Do not be fooled into believing that superficial changes are significant. Be prepared for the "implementation dip." Finally, the process provides many benefits. Some are surprising.

Time

Not surprisingly, time is the most precious resource in the planning process. Most educators already find themselves overburdened and short on time (Reese, 2006). To add a process that requires more time seems almost absurd. However, the need for strategic planning is so critical that the time has to be found. Teachers most closely engaged with change efforts spend about 23 days a year, or 13 percent of their time, on reform (Fullan and Miles, 1992). Everyone can try to increase the present efficiency of his regular responsibilities, but some functions will have to receive a lower priority, at least for the first year.

Money

It is difficult to predict how much will be required by a given school. Most of it will go for professional development and external assistance (Dunsworth and Billings, 2009, 113–115).

Support of the Administration

The strategic planning process must be enthusiastically supported by the superintendent or another key decision maker. Since strategic planning seems to be most successful when it is site based, the building principal should also be a vital part of the process. Ideally, both should be involved; at least one *has* to be. Teachers will not invest their time and energy when they see that strategic planning is not being promoted by key educational leaders in their school and district (Conley, 1992).

Superficial Changes

Although superficial changes may be appropriate for minor problems, real change can come about only when the significant issues are dealt with. If the vision statement has been developed as proposed herein, it will address the heart of the educational process. Consequently, the closer the action plans are to that vision, the more complex they will probably be. As Fullan and Miles note, "The assertive pursuit of problems in the service of continuous improvement is the kind of accountability that can make a difference" (1992, 750).

"Implementation Dip"

The mystic St. John of the Cross used to refer to the fallow periods of his prayer life as the "dark night of the soul." So too will there be what Fullan and Miles call an "implementation dip" during the strategic planning process. This is that time when seemingly nothing is going right for the team. Even in those cases where reform eventually succeeds, things will often go wrong before they go right (Fullan and Miles, 1992). When the planning team reaches out to the greater community, it is accused of being intrusive. When the members pull back in self-defense, they are called aloof and elitist. This usually happens because the changes they are proposing represent new meaning and new learning. As stated before in discussing the change process, these reactions are predictable and painful. The hostility from various constituent groups will be amazingly strident at times (Curran, 1991). There may be accusations that the process is not being conducted in an open and honest manner (Conley, 1992). However, these are signs that significant change is being attempted (Fullan and Miles, 1992).

Because strategic planning in the educational setting is an inclusive process, most of the criticisms against it have to do with involvement (or exclusion) and communication (Conley, 1992). Even though the implementation dip seems to be inevitable, the best way out of it is to include more of those who wish to participate and to develop new channels of communication.

Benefits

Although most planning groups enter strategic planning as a rational process to identify what needs to be done, an unexpected outcome is that it brings with it social and political benefits. Thus, although action plans are the most obvious outcomes, many participants report that it may have even greater value in providing a means to get groups to communicate, to appreciate varying points of view, and to provide a general direction for the school (Conley, 1992). There is not much research to support this aspect of strategic planning, but my own experiences tend to reaffirm this notion. Even though the deep problems are not yet solved, an *esprit de corps* is built up while attempting to come up with answers. Teams learn to experiment, make decisions, and collaborate. This leads to improved interpersonal skills, opening up of dialogue, and greater empowerment (Curran, 1991). Strategic planning brings with it the benefits of sharing ideas, successes, and problems with others. Ideas are exchanged and built upon. Professional colleagues can give the necessary emotional support for risk taking (Curran, 1991).

Parents appear to be strongest in believing that strategic planning will lead to an improved school (Conley, 1992). If this attitude continues during the implementation process, strategic planning will have tremendous political and public relations value.

By a convincing margin, labor relations improve where strategic planning has been employed. It provides a forum where teachers and administrators can find a common cause and purpose (Conley, 1992).

Last, even if the process is abandoned or put in "mothballs," it will have done the following:

1. Employed data in order to study the way the school functions.

2. Involved a wide range of people in the decision-making process.

3. Taught people to set goals and direction for the school.

4. Developed action planning teams to consider the best way to achieve a goal.

5. Devised a monitoring process for action plans. (Conley, 1992)

These activities will create a new perspective on what an educator or community member can do to improve a school.

The benefits to the school librarian can be many. He can be viewed as the educator who helped turn the planning process into an information-rich experience. He can be seen as a fellow decision maker. He can help point the school in the direction of information access. He can be viewed as "owning" one or more action plans. Finally, he can show other members ways of organizing and tracking action plans. All these involvements are vital to the success of the planning process.

CHAPTER 23

Conclusion

Educators who employ strategic planning have available a powerful tool to meet the rising pressure to make American schools world class. Because it is ongoing, comprehensive, inclusive, and systematic, it is an approach particularly suited to schools. It is ongoing or continuous because it must adapt to a changing world. It is comprehensive because its vision-making process keeps all parties focused on the larger picture. Because of the social structure of most schools, any major change is eventually going to have to be embraced by the entire school community. Strategic planning, by being inclusive, derives much of its energy from the enthusiasm of its participants. Last, its systematic, or rational, aspects, which are centered in its vision, mission, and action plans, bring to a school a means of combating the pressures and special interests that tend to pull it apart.

Because the process is relatively straightforward, it can be employed in most school settings. Although there is usually some confusion in the beginning over the distinction among its parts (e.g., vision vs. mission), none of its elements is so specialized that a planning team could not fathom them. Outside consultants can and should be used to help initiate and sustain the process. However, the plan will be unique to the individuals who make up the team and the greater school community.

Although there will inevitably be low points, or dips, during the planning process, the benefits of attempting to plan strategically are so numerous and significant that it becomes a highly worthwhile exercise, even if it is not sustained. By going through external scanning, internal scanning, and organizational analysis, the school will have systematically employed data to examine the way it functions. By developing a vision and a mission and by writing action plans, it will have set goals and a direction for the school. By devising a means to monitor action plans, it will have shown that it could devise a system to do this. Finally, strategic planning involves all members of the school community. In so doing, it gives them a new perspective on what is involved in educating children and how they might be a part of the restructuring of education.

The Place of the School Librarian in Strategic Planning

Although school librarians are not often part of school or district planning teams, they should be considered essential to the success of the planning process. School librarians are among the very few educators who realize, daily, the importance of timely and accurate information about the outside world (external scanning). They are used to regularly analyzing data (internal scanning). Since they do not represent an academic department, they are usually very aware of the strengths and weaknesses of the entire school (organizational analysis). With the world of information changing so rapidly, the school librarian is forced to develop a vision of how the library will fit into that milieu. Supported by initiatives such as *Empowering Learners*, the school librarian knows that part of the mission of a school is to develop competent and informed consumers of information. Finally, the school librarian develops action plans regularly to perform the many tasks and services required to run the library. Strategic planning is an unusually rare opportunity for the school librarian to become a leader in the movement to restructure education.

Bibliography

Banathy, Bela. *Systems Design of Education: Journey to Create the Future.* Englewood Cliffs, NJ: Educational Technology Publications, 1991.

Cohen, Allan R., and David L. Bradford. "The Influence Model: Using Reciprocity and Exchange to Get What You Need." *Journal of Organizational Excellence*, Winter 2005.

Conley, David T. "Strategic Planning in America's Schools: An Exploratory Study." Paper presented at the annual meeting of the American Educational Research Association. San Francisco, CA, 1992.

Curran, Anne B. "Visions That Guide Change: Final Report of the ASCD Restructuring Consortium." Alexandria, VA: Association for Supervision and Curriculum Development, 1991.

Curry, Marnie. "Critical Friends Groups: The Possibilities and Limitations Embedded in Teacher Professional Communities Aimed at Instructional Improvement and School Reform." *Teachers College Record* 110.4 (2008): 733. Platinum Periodicals, ProQuest. Web. July 25, 2010.

Dunsworth, Mardale, and Dawn L. Billings. *The High-Performing School: Benchmarking the 10 Indicators of Effectiveness.* Bloomington, IN: Solution Tree Press, 2009.

Eisenberg, Michael, and Robert Berkowitz. *Big6™ Skills Approach to Library & Information Skills Instruction.* Norwood, NJ: Ablex Publishing, 1990.

Empowering Learners: Guidelines for School Library Media Programs. Chicago, IL: American Association of School Librarians, 2009.

Fullan, Michael. "Innovation, Reform, and Restructuring Strategies," *Challenges and Achievements of American Education. 1993 Yearbook of the Association for Supervision and Curriculum Development.* Alexandria, VA: Association for Supervision and Curriculum Development, 1993, 116–133.

Fullan, Michael. "The Three Stories of Education Reform." *Phi Delta Kappan* 81.8 (2000): 581–584. Platinum Periodicals, ProQuest. Web. July 25, 2010.

Fullan, Michael. "The Change Leader." *Educational Leadership* May 1, 2002: Platinum Periodicals, ProQuest. Web. July 25, 2010.

Fullan, Michael G., and Matthew B. Miles. "Getting Reform Right: What Works and What Doesn't," *Phi Delta Kappan* (June, 1992): 745–752.

Halberstam, David. *The Fifties.* New York: Villard Books, 1993.

Hall, Gene E., and Shirley M. Hord. *Change in Schools: Facilitating the Process.* Albany: State University of New York Press, 1984.

Haycock, Ken. "Teacher-Librarians-Continuing to Build," *Canadian Library Journal* (February, 1985): 27–33.

Hill, Paul T., and Bonan, Josephine, "Site-Based Management: Decentralization and Accountability," *Education Digest*, 23–25 (September 1991).

Joyce, Bruce, James Wolf, and Emily Calhoun. *The Self-Renewing School.* Alexandria, VA: Association for Supervision and Curriculum Development, 1993.

Kaplan, George R., and Michael D. Usdan. "The Changing Look of Education's Policy Networks," *Phi Delta Kappan* (May 1992): 664–672.

Kilbane, J. "Factors in Sustaining Professional Learning Community." *National Association of Secondary School Principals. NASSP Bulletin,* September 1, 2009: Platinum Periodicals, ProQuest. Web. July 25, 2010.

Leon, R., and S. Davis. "Great Leaders for Great Schools." *Leadership,* September 1, 2009: Platinum Periodicals, ProQuest. Web. July 25, 2010.

Loertscher, D. "Curriculum, the Library/Learning Commons, and Teacher-Librarians: Myths and Realities in the Second Decade." *Teacher Librarian* 37.3 (2010): 8–13. Platinum Periodicals, ProQuest. Web. July 25, 2010.

Loertscher, David V. "Objective: Achievement, Solution: School Libraries," *School Library Journal* (May 1993): 30–33.

Loertscher, David V. *Taxonomies of the School Library Media Program* San Jose, CA: Hi Willow Research and Publishing, 2000.

Menzie, Sue. Sandwich Leadership: Leading from the Middle. January 2008–July 24, 2010. http://www.tapestryleadershipconcepts.com/articles/sandwich

Morrison, Samuel Eliot. *Admiral of the Ocean Sea*: *A Life of Christopher Columbus.* Boston: Little, Brown and Co., 1942.

The National Academies. The Concerns-Based Adoption Model (CBAM): A Model for Change in Individuals. 2005–July 24, 2010. http://www.nationalacademies.org/rise/backg4a.htm

National Association of Secondary School Principals. *Breaking Ranks II: Strategies for Leading High School Reform.* Reston, VA: National Association of Secondary School Principals, 2004.

O'Neil, John, "Systems Change Seen for Schools," *ASCD Update,* 1+ (June 1993).

Partnership for 21st Century Skills. Framework for 21st Century Learning. http://www.p21.org/index.php?option=com_content&task=view&id=254&Itemid=119

Perelman, Lewis J., "Restructuring the System is the Solution," *Phi Delta Kappan*, 21 (September 1988).

Reese, Susan. October 2006. Time Management for Administrators. *Techniques,* 81(7), 10–11. Retrieved July 26, 2010, from Platinum Periodicals. (Document ID: 1143278561)

Rogers, JoAnn V. "Real Information Power," *School Library Journal* (March 1993): 113–117.

Saphier, Jon, Tom Bigda-Payton, and Geoff Pierson. *How to Make Decisions That Stay Made.* Alexandria, VA: Association for Supervision and Curriculum Development, 1989.

Sherman, W. "Are Librarians Totally Obsolete? 33 Reasons Why Libraries and Librarians Are Still Extremely Important." *Teacher Librarian* 35.1 (2007): 21–27. Platinum Periodicals, ProQuest. Web. July 25, 2010.

Shook, Robert L. *Honda: An American Success Story.* New York: Prentice Hall, 1988.

Teacher Librarian Ning. 2010. Joyce Valenza. http://teacherlibrarian.ning.com/

Zmuda, A., and V. Harada. (2008). Librarians as Learning Specialists: Moving from the Margins to the Mainstream of School Leadership. *Teacher Librarian,* 36(1): 15–20. Retrieved July 26, 2010, from Platinum Periodicals. (Document ID: 1597327351)

Index